CAPITALISM IS EXTINCTION SOCIALISM IS SURVIVAL

The climate crisis no solution under capitalism

CONTENTS

a pamphlet by

FIGHT RACISM!

FIGHT IMPERIALISM!

Contributions from Charles Chinweizu, Robert Clough,
Susan Davidson, Adam Grey, Trevor Rayne and Nathan Williams.
Edited by Suzi Rose.
An **FRFI** pamphlet

Published by Larkin Publications
BCM Box 5909, London, WC1N 3XX

www.frfi.org.uk

ISBN 10: 0-905400-32-1
ISBN 13: 978-0-905400-32-7

Cover design: Grace Kress www.shelbyxstudios.com
Design and typesetting: Joe Smith

In memory of our comrade Trevor Rayne, 1949 – 2022, a member of the Revolutionary Communist Group and author of many Fight Racism! Fight Imperialism! articles on multinationals, the environment and imperialism. A communist and anti-imperialist, he contributed greatly to the struggle for environmental and social justice.

PREFACE

This pamphlet was prepared by the environmental subcommittee of the Revolutionary Communist Group (RCG). It explains how capitalist production, and imperialist exploitation, necessarily result in environmental destruction and has generated the climate crisis which threatens extinction for our planet. Imperialist states use war, military occupation and conflict to drive forward production for profit, trampling any obstacles in their way. The pamphlet also explains why socialism is the only way forward for the planet and people to survive.

INTRODUCTION

Marx showed that labour and nature are the sources of wealth, and that under capitalism both nature and the worker are exploited in the interests of capital accumulation. In capitalist production, nature is seen as a free gift to capital. Driven by the profit motive, the capitalist is only interested in the unlimited expansion of capital. Natural resources like land, water, raw materials and hydrocarbons are only of interest to the capitalist in so far as they can be turned into profit. It is the logic of the system of capitalist production, not specific policy decisions, which makes capitalism unsustainable. In the 19th century, Marx observed in Britain both a loss in soil fertility and workers living in overcrowded polluted cities, with precarious livelihoods. Today we see catastrophic global warming and fuel shortages, with the mass of humanity living in permanent underdevelopment, while a small minority live unsustainable consumerist lifestyles.

The interactions between human societies and the natural world are at the centre of the productive process in each historical period. Under the capitalist mode of production both nature and human labour power are exploited in an insatiable drive for profit. The climate crisis which today threatens the world is not the result of a 'new kind' of capitalism, as some claim, but the inevitable result of capitalism itself. The private appropriation of social wealth leads to damage on a global scale as the production of wealth for the private sector generates environmental and communal destruction across the globe. A mere 100 companies are now responsible for 71% of the deadly emissions that lead to planetary ruin and contribute to mass poverty.

Marx understood the capitalist mode of production as a matter of class power and class antagonism. Capitalism has an immanent drive and a constant tendency to revolutionise labour productivity. Around the world, the working class, proletarianised people and indigenous communities are those who suffer most. Marx also argued that socialism is needed to overcome the human alienation from nature that exists under capitalism. We need to move entirely away from a profit-driven economy to a socialist planned economy to escape this dictatorship of the wealthy owners of our planet if we are to survive sustainably and meet the needs of the whole of humanity.

Profit versus the planet

Capitalism's tendency to destroy the very foundations of life lies in the nature of the system itself. All modes of production, all applications of human labour to nature, consume and exhaust natural resources. But under capitalism, with its massive productive powers and pursuit of profits, this process assumes a qualitatively more intense and destructive character, which is beyond social control and which outstrips the capacity of the natural world to renew itself. Production for profit requires cheap raw materials on a vast scale; it requires growth and expansion constrained by no social needs. To this end it has developed mass consumer markets and 'throw-away' products, while its advertising agents specialise in cultivating new and wasteful needs. To stay competitive, capitalists seek to reduce to a minimum all costs not directly generating a profit and thus will evade environmental protection costs as they do the costs of ensuring health and safety for their workers.

Today capitalist social relations threaten the world with disaster. As Marx said:

> *'At a certain stage of development, the material productive forces of society come into conflict with the existing relations of production. From forms of development of the productive forces these relations turn into their fetters.'*[1]

1 Karl Marx, from the preface to *A Contribution to the Critique of Political Economy*, Progress Publishers, Moscow, 1977.

Capitalist relations have now become more than a 'fetter' (a constraint); they have become a death threat to humanity. Today the world economy is dominated by huge banks and corporations. With branches in hundreds of countries they control every stage of production from mining raw materials to the marketing of the end product. Planning production on vast scales, they have more power than many a government, and their decisions affect the lives of billions of people. This is imperialism. The purpose is the enrichment of a small number of financiers and private businesses, disregarding the needs of the world's population. Whilst production remains under the control of monopoly private interests it is directly opposed to the interests of humanity and to the proper, conscious and socially planned stewardship of the Earth's resources and the harmonious development of society and its natural environment.

Britain's role

Britain is the oldest capitalist country in the world. It is the birthplace of the industrial revolution which relied on large-scale fossil fuel combustion and development of heavy industry. Today it is a parasitic imperialist power. For centuries, the British ruling class has extracted profits from its overseas 'assets'; it has privatised natural resources, destroyed communities, exploited populations and plundered their natural habitats.[2] While most of the underdeveloped world is now formally independent, Britain continues to exert imperialist domination through ownership and control of resources, markets and finances across the world. Imperialism is the economic driver behind the imbalanced global economy, where so much is wasted by the rich while the poor struggle to survive. It is the driver of unrelenting environmental destruction.

In this pamphlet we examine the environmental crisis which threatens the futures of everyone.

2 For a further discussion this see David Yaffe, 'Globalisation, parasitic and decaying capitalism', *Fight Racism! Fight Imperialism!* (FRFI) 158 December 2000 / January 2001.

Chapter 1 provides a scientific explanation of global warming and climate change. It explains why mitigating or adapting to, let alone reversing, the effects of climate change are impossible under capitalism.

Chapter 2 gives an overview of world summits on the environment. We show that from the first Intergovernmental Panel on Climate Change in 1988, to the recent Conference of the Parties (COP26) in 2021, there has been no serious commitment to a coordinated global response to the climate crisis.

Chapter 3 focuses on the environment and imperialism, describing the devastating impact of multinational corporations on the environment and communities worldwide.

Chapter 4 shows that there is no 'green' solution under capitalism, debunking the myths of the 'Green New Deal' lobby and the 'Degrowth' movement. The project of sustainable capitalism is doomed from the start because maximising profit and saving the planet are irreconcilable goals.

Chapter 5 presents an account of the resistance movements in Britain to environmental destruction.

Chapter 6 illustrates that socialism is the only possible solution to the environmental crisis, and therefore to our survival. There are important precedents from the Soviet Union that we can learn from in terms of socialist state planning. Cuba today leads on environmental protection and sustainable development. It is an example for the rest of the world to follow.

South London Fight Racism! Fight Imperialism! (FRFI) Cop26? Cop Out! Protest, Peckham, November 2021

one
THE SCIENCE
of global warming and climate change

Global warming

The scientific evidence for global warming is unequivocal: Earth's average surface temperature has increased by 1.18°C (above the baseline of 14°C) since the end of the 19th century. Global surface temperatures are the warmest in over 100,000 years. The rate of global warming is unprecedented in the last 2,000 years, and a 2013 study showed it is now higher than it has been for most (90%) of the last 11,300 years. Recent global average temperature rises are so abrupt that charts of the data show the line of increase is nearly vertical.[3]

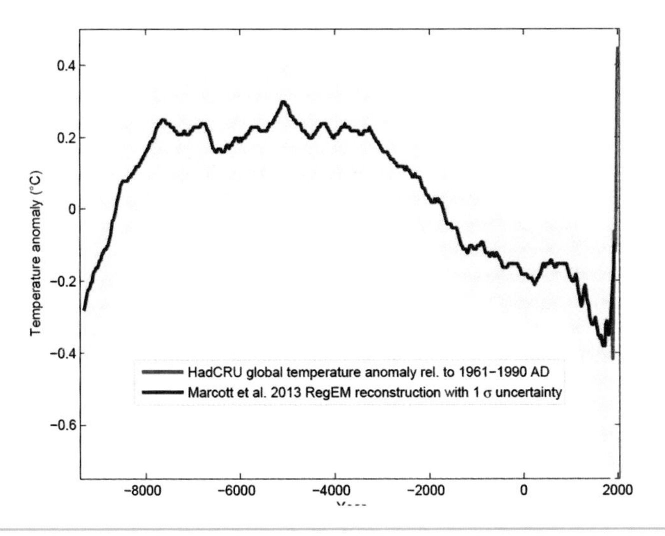

3 Graph showing anomalous temperatures during the 'holocene' from OSS Foundation, www.ossfoundation.us

Current global warming is occurring roughly ten times faster than the average rate of Ice-Age-recovery warming, and is too rapid to be linked to changes in Earth's orbit, and too large to be caused by solar activity. The claim that the Sun alone is responsible for global warming as a natural phenomenon is disproved by the fact there has been no upward trend in the amount of the Sun's energy reaching Earth since 1978. We would also expect to see warming throughout all layers of the atmosphere if the Sun were responsible. Instead, scientists observe warming at the surface and cooling in the upper atmosphere (stratosphere), which is consistent with the warming being caused by a build-up of heat-trapping gases near the surface of the Earth.

Carbon dioxide (CO_2) and other trace gases contained in the atmosphere, such as water vapour, ozone, methane, carbon monoxide, oxides of nitrogen, chlorofluorocarbons and 15 minor halogenated gases trap and absorb part of the infrared radiation from the Sun that are re-radiated by the Earth. This increase in absorbed energy warms the atmosphere, inducing warming at the Earth's surface. This phenomenon is referred to as the 'greenhouse effect'. As the concentration of these gases increases, more warming than would naturally occur happens. The United Nations Intergovernmental Panel on Climate Change (IPCC), a group of 230 independent scientific experts from across the world, reported in August 2021 that:

> *'It is unequivocal that human influence has warmed the atmosphere, ocean and land. Widespread and rapid changes in the atmosphere, ocean, cryosphere and biosphere have occurred... [and] increases in well-mixed greenhouse gas concentrations since around 1750 are unequivocally caused by human activities.'*[4]

The IPCC predicted global average warming is 'very likely to reach 1.0-1.8°C' by 2081-2100 even with net zero emissions by 2050. Staying

---

4 IPCC, 'Climate Change 2021: The Physical Science Basis', 2021, www.ipcc.ch

at current rates of emissions until 2050, warming could reach 2.1-3.5°C by 2100, and 3.3-5.7°C by 2100 if emissions rate doubled. The second part of the IPCC's report published in February 2022 confirmed this assessment and issued its bleakest warning yet on the impact of rising temperatures on communities around the world.

Ratcliffe-on-Soar Power Station, Nottinghamshire

Greenhouse gases

The build-up of atmospheric carbon dioxide has been systematically monitored by the National Oceanic and Atmospheric Administration's Observatory in Hawaii since 1957, and has coincided with the start of the capitalist industrial revolution at the beginning of the 19th century. The burning of fossil fuels like coal, oil and natural gas, and to a lesser extent deforestation for agriculture, urbanisation and industry, have increased the concentration of carbon dioxide and other greenhouse gases in the atmosphere. The burning process combines carbon with oxygen in the air to make CO_2. Economic activities that the imperialist system depends upon have raised atmospheric carbon dioxide levels from 280 parts per million (ppm) to 410 ppm over the last 150 years. Carbon dioxide levels today are higher than at any point in at least the past 800,000 years. CO_2 levels, which were rising at 0.6 ppm per year in the 1960s, rose by 2.3 ppm per year between 2009 and 2018. An internal report by oil giant Exxon's Coordination and Planning Division in April 1982 projected CO_2 levels reaching 540 ppm by 2050 with average global surface temperature increases exceeding 2°C. On current trends atmospheric CO_2 is projected to exceed 900 ppm by 2100.[5]

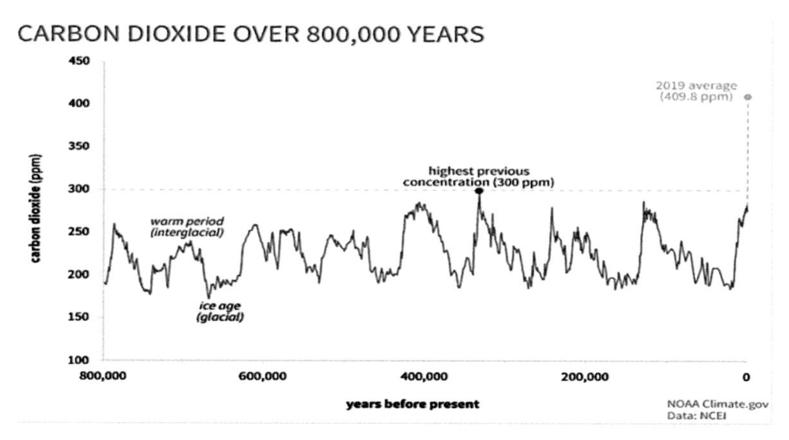

CO_2 is the most important of Earth's 'long-lived' greenhouse gases because it remains semi-permanently (more than 100 years) in the atmosphere, not responding physically or chemically to changes in temperature, hence 'forcing' climate change. About 50% of the greenhouse effect is due to water vapour, 25% due to clouds, 20% to CO_2, with other gases accounting for the remainder. But although CO_2 absorbs less heat per molecule than methane or nitrous oxide, it absorbs energy that water vapour does not, which means it adds to the greenhouse effect in a unique way.

Increases in atmospheric carbon dioxide are responsible for about two-thirds of the total energy imbalance which causes global warming. 33% of CO_2 emissions also dissolve into the oceans causing ocean acidification and lowering the ocean's pH. Since 1850 the pH of the ocean's surface has dropped from 8.21 to 8.10, which may not seem like much, but the pH scale is logarithmic. A 1.0 unit drop in pH equals a ten-fold increase, so a 0.1-unit fall means a 26% increase in ocean acidity, adding to the threat to marine life.

In addition, 90% of the extra heat energy from global warming has also been absorbed by the oceans, with surface temperatures rising 0.3°C since

5 Graph from NOAA climate.gov

1969. This has led to coral-reef bleaching and dieback. The IPCC says 'global warming of 2°C or more would lead to 99% of corals being lost',[6] and a 2020 study revealed coral cover across the Caribbean declined by 80% from 1977 to 2001 and may completely disappear by 2035.

As the oceans warm, they also expand, leading to a rise in sea levels. The IPCC reports that global mean sea levels increased by 0.2m between 1901 and 2018, and the average rate increase accelerated from 1.3mm per year between 1901 and 1971, to 1.9mm per year between 1971 and 2006, further increasing to 3.7mm per year between 2006 and 2018. Global warming will not be evenly spread over the globe; greater warming will occur at higher latitudes; the polar ice caps could experience warming of up to 10°C and the Equator little if any. The North Pole had already experienced average warming up to 3°C by 2014.

Melting ice in the Arctic, 2021

The most abundant greenhouse gas, water vapour, has little direct effect on climate and does not 'radiatively force' climate change like CO_2; rather, it acts as 'feedback': as CO_2 levels rise, the atmosphere warms and the amount of water vapour in the atmosphere increases as surface water evaporates. This slowly increases the greenhouse effect, trapping more heat on the Earth's surface. The atmosphere warms further, causing more water vapour to be held in the atmosphere, and so on in an accelerating 'positive feedback loop'. Water vapour also condenses to form clouds which can add

6 'IPCC, op cit.'

to the greenhouse effect by trapping heat in the atmosphere (high clouds), or, alternatively, as low clouds reduce the warming by reflecting energy back to space, cooling the planet.

Methane is a key trace greenhouse gas. Its concentration in the atmosphere at 1,866 parts per billion (ppb) in 2019 has doubled since 1850 primarily due to agriculture (livestock rearing) and leaks from fossil fuel use such as hydraulic fracturing (fracking). Methane lingers for 12 years in the atmosphere but it is more than 20 times as potent as CO_2 as a greenhouse gas: over 100 years, one tonne of methane is still equivalent to about 28 tonnes of CO_2. Over a 20-year period, the effect is even greater according to the IPCC: the global warming potential of one tonne of atmospheric methane is similar to that of around 85 tonnes of CO_2. Although bacteria in natural wetlands produce methane when decomposing organic material, emissions from wetlands or other natural sources have not increased substantially since 2000, while industrial agriculture and the fossil fuel industry together account for 40-50% of global methane emissions. In 2017, a record 596 million tonnes of methane were emitted globally, 227 million tonnes by industrial agriculture and 108 million tonnes by the fossil fuel industry. Methane is also involved in a positive feedback loop: methane is trapped in frozen peat bogs, permafrost and as 'water ice' (solid methane hydrates) under the sea floor. As atmospheric and ocean temperatures increase, the peat bogs and methane hydrates will thaw, releasing more methane. This will in turn cause greater global warming, more thawing, and the release of more methane.

The rate of carbon dioxide emissions is also disturbing the global carbon cycle which has been in equilibrium for millennia relatively undisturbed from the last Ice Age 12,000 years ago up to the capitalist industrial revolution. Carbon is in constant flux between the atmosphere and the terrestrial biosphere, and the atmosphere and the oceans. Carbon dioxide in the atmosphere is in intimate contact with the oceans which can process it and hence absorb large quantities of it. This happens over many centuries. The oceans can ultimately absorb about 95% of human-made

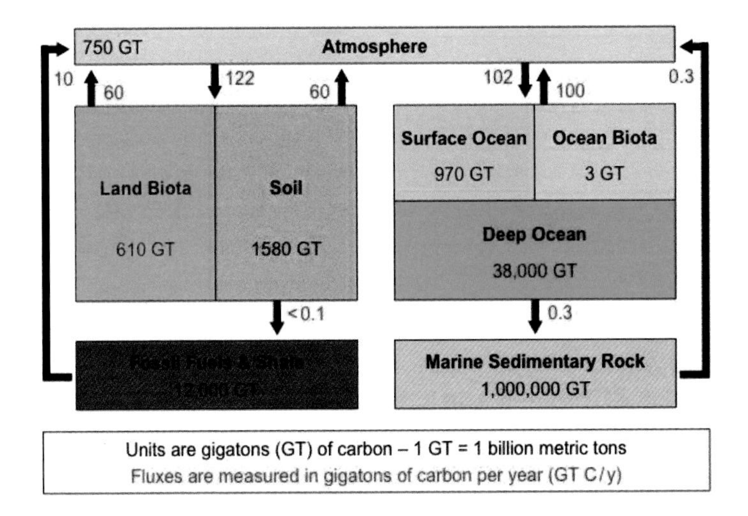

carbon emissions. The diagram[7] shows the importance of the oceans as a sink for atmospheric carbon dioxide: they are the largest such carbon reservoir.

The atmospheric reservoir of carbon is estimated at about 750 gigatonnes of carbon (GtC), with the oceans holding almost 39,000 GtC; the terrestrial biosphere holds almost 2,200 GtC. The land biota (flora and fauna) holds nearly 610 GtC and the soil about 1,600 GtC. The man-made CO_2 emissions estimated at 10 GtC annually (up from 6GtC/year in the 1990s and from 8GtC/year in 2006) are the only ones that have disturbed the balance of the equilibrium of carbon fluxes believed to have existed for millennia. The absorptive capacity of the oceans trails considerably behind the rate of current CO_2 emissions. In fact, the oceans in preindustrial times were actually a net source of carbon, releasing 0.6 GtC/year into the atmosphere, but the rate of anthropogenic emissions under capitalism has forced a reverse situation, turning the oceans into a net carbon sink which between 1992 and 2018 have probably absorbed 67bn tonnes of CO_2, or almost 3bn tonnes annually.

7 Diagram of global carbon fluxes from BioNinja, www.ib.bioninja.com.au

Deforestation

With 12,000 GtC in the form of fossil fuels available for industrial use, we can also see that the atmosphere could be easily overwhelmed. No amount of tree planting, even a doubling of current land biota, can solve the problem of carbon emissions, if the capitalists continue at the current rate. Along with the oceans, forests act as a 'sink' for carbon dioxide, and absorb the majority of carbon emissions. But the clearing of forests is now also a primary source of CO_2 emissions. Forests occupied four billion hectares (38%) of habitable land (10.6 billion hectares) in 2018. Forests are being lost at an increasing rate, with 80 million hectares lost since 1990, and 1.1 billion hectares lost since 1900. Every year between 2011 and 2015 about 20 million hectares of forest were cut down. Since 2016, this has increased to an annual average of 28 million hectares.

Rainforest loss has devastating consequences for the climate, for forest-dwelling people and for biodiversity. Demand for land on which to produce palm oil, soy, rubber, beef and leather in the Amazon, Southeast Asia and Central Africa helped drive an estimated 23 million hectares of tropical forest loss between 2016 and 2020 – an area nearly the size of the United Kingdom.

2.2% of the global greenhouse gas emissions in 2016 came from deforestation when 49.5 billion tonnes of CO_2 were emitted. If 0.7% (28 million hectares) of forests, which together hold about 1,200 GtC in timber and soil, are cut down annually, this could contribute 8.4 Gt of CO_2 to the atmosphere annually. In 2019, when 43 GtC of global emissions are estimated to have arisen from all human activity, almost 15% (6.2 GtC) came from land use changes which include deforestation and forest fires, while fossil fuels and industry were responsible for the rest (36.8 GtC). The Global Carbon Project estimates about 44% of CO_2 emitted in 2019 will accumulate in the atmosphere, with the rest absorbed by the terrestrial biosphere (33%) and the oceans (22%).

Agribusiness is the immediate driver for around 80% of deforestation worldwide; the unsustainable demand for agricultural products in imperialist countries is driving deforestation. The clearing of land for the rearing of livestock (mainly beef), is responsible for driving deforestation. 63 million hectares were cleared between 1990 and 2008 for beef; 13 million hectares for soybean; eight million hectares for maize; six million hectares for palm oil and five million hectares for wood.

Deforestation at the Guatemala-Belize border

Tipping points

An increase in absorbed energy via the greenhouse effect warming the Earth's surface causes changes in the climate, affecting atmospheric and ocean temperatures, rainfall patterns, soil moisture and potentially melting the polar ice caps. At some point these small incremental changes to global temperatures, atmospheric CO_2 levels, ocean acidification and rising sea levels, as well as the self-reinforcing feedback loops, could lead to irreversible 'tipping points'. Once such a threshold has been crossed, a further tiny change could push the 'tipping element' into a completely new, unstable, unpredictable and, crucially, uncontrollable state.[8] Several 'tipping elements' have been identified:

- Melting of the Arctic sea ice and ice sheets: sea ice has large white surfaces which reflect solar radiation away from Earth. This reflectivity, called 'albedo', reduces as sea ice melts, exposing the much darker ocean surface beneath, which absorbs more radiation rather than reflecting it. This, in turn, amplifies warming, leading

8 This section is drawn from the 'Tipping Points' series of articles on the Carbon Brief website at www.carbonbrief.org

to more melting in a vicious feedback cycle. Even if Arctic sea ice melting may not be a tipping element, it could have hidden feedback effects on other tipping elements that are as yet unknown.

- The Greenland ice sheet is the second largest mass of ice on Earth, holding enough water to raise global sea levels by 7.2 metres. Its disintegration would change the shape of the world's coastlines. NASA's Gravity Recovery and Climate Experiment shows Greenland lost an average of 279 billion tonnes of ice per year between 1993 and 2019. As these ice sheets irreversibly melt and retreat, sea levels rise, leading to the flooding of coastal land areas. Meltwater from the ice sheet has been adding to sea levels by 0.7mm per year and the IPCC says that once underway its decay would be 'irreversible for millennia'. Large sea-ice and ice sheets loss may reach a critical, irreversible threshold.
- The West Antarctic Ice Sheet (WAIS) is one of three regions making up Antarctica. The rate of ice loss from WAIS had tripled from 53 billion tonnes a year between 1992 and 1997 to 159 billion tonnes a year in 2012-2017, with a consequent measurable rise in sea levels.
- Arctic warming and Greenland meltwater are driving an influx of fresh water into the North Atlantic. This could have contributed to a 15% slowdown since the mid-20th century of the Atlantic Meridional Overturning Circulation (AMOC), the ocean circulation 'conveyor belt' which transports warm ocean water and heat from the Pacific Ocean via the African Cape towards Europe and Greenland. An input of freshwater makes the ocean less salty and less heavy, reducing the amount of 'deep water' produced and slowing down the ocean conveyor belt. A shutdown of AMOC would cause widespread cooling around the whole of the northern hemisphere, in the order of several degrees, possibly 5°C, impact on rainfall patterns, and lead to losses of agricultural output. The whole Atlantic ecosystem could be disrupted, which in turn could trigger other tipping elements such as the naturally-occurring phenomenon in the Pacific, known as El Niño/La Niña. During El Niño, the oceans release heat into the

atmosphere causing those years to be the hottest on record. La Niña tends to drag temperatures down. An AMOC shutdown could cause changes in the El Niño-Southern Oscillation characteristics, dieback of the Amazon rainforest and shrinking of the WAIS ice sheet.

Deforestation in the Brazilian Amazon

- Another tipping element is the 'Amazon Forest dieback': The Amazon rainforest in Latin America is the largest in the world, twice the size of India, and a habitat for millions of species of plants, insects, birds and animals. It creates half its own rainfall through evaporation of moisture through leaves (transpiration). Increased levels of CO_2, sea level rises and changes in rainfall patterns, as well as widespread deforestation mean that at some tipping point the Amazon would no longer be able to sustain itself and would 'dieback' to a drier ecosystem such as a savannah. This would be a catastrophe for Amazonian wildlife. A February 2020 BBC *Newsnight* report indicated that parts of the Amazon may already have reached this tipping point: 'Dry seasons in Amazonian regions are already hotter and longer. Mortality rates of wet climate species are increased, whereas dry climate species are showing resilience. The increasing frequency of unprecedented droughts in 2005, 2010, 2015 and 2016 is signalling that the tipping point is at hand.'[9] 17% of the Amazon has been lost since 1970, and deforestation has increased

9 BBC, 'Is the Amazon rainforest beyond saving?' *Newsnight*, February 2020.

rapidly since 2018 under Brazil's President Jair Bolsonaro, who is backed by both British and US imperialism. The tipping point for Amazon dieback could lie in the range 20-40% of forest loss. This would influence weather patterns globally, and would mean the loss of an important carbon dioxide sink, accelerating global warming. In fact, the south-eastern part – around 20% of the Amazon basin – has become a net source of CO_2.

- The West African monsoon is another tipping element. Between the late 1960s and 1980s, a lack of rain affected the Sahel, with average rainfall declining by more than 30% over most of the region compared to the 1950s. This plunged the region into an extended drought, although the attendant famines were caused primarily by the agriculturally destructive character of the International Monetary Fund's (IMF) structural adjustment programmes. A 2003 study showed that the source of the droughts lay primarily in warming sea surface temperatures in the tropical oceans around Africa. The rising sea surface temperatures push the monsoon rains southwards away from the Sahel, creating drought conditions. Cooling caused by air pollution from northern hemisphere countries also contributed to the droughts, as did falling 'climate-vegetation feedback', where drier conditions saw less vegetation growth, a reduction in evapo-transpiration and even less rainfall. Neither traditional farming techniques nor an expanding local population were regarded as contributory factors.
- Permafrost – soil or rock containing ice or frozen organic material that has remained at or below 0°C for at least two years – is found in large areas of Siberia, Alaska, Canada, Patagonia, New Zealand's Southern Alps and Antarctica. It holds vast amounts of carbon accumulated from dead plants and animals over thousands of years. As Carbon Brief explains: 'as the climate warms, there is an increasing risk that that permafrost will thaw…This process releases CO_2 and – to a lesser extent – methane. [This] has the potential to cause further climate warming.' There is evidence that

permafrost is already thawing and 'across the Arctic "could be releasing an estimated 300-600m tonnes of net carbon per year to the atmosphere".' We can stop the warming and thawing of permafrost but once the carbon is released there is no getting it back into the permafrost. These changes are irreversible.

- Boreal forests make up 30% of the world's forests and are found in the cold climes of the Arctic in Russia and Canada. Due to global warming the boreal biome is warming rapidly, shifting to a sparsely wooded or grassland ecosystem, with high tree mortality, increased diseases and reduced reproduction, more frequent and intense forests fires and dieback. A 2012 study of forests in Alaska has already shown a 'widespread shift from coniferous to deciduous vegetation [that] began around 1990'. Underneath the boreal forests is the permafrost. As the ice sheets retreat and boreal forests expand northwards, the albedo decreases, causing the land underneath to absorb more solar radiation. In addition, permafrost previously frozen under the boreal forests or ice sheets could also thaw, leading to more warming as methane is released, which in turn leads to more forest degradation, a potential double-whammy for carbon emissions: increased emissions and fewer trees to absorb it.
- The melting of billions of tonnes of ice held in the world's glaciers has caused marked shifts in Earth's axis of rotation since the 1990s, as the Earth's mass is redistributed around the globe. In consequence, the North and South Poles have drifted in new directions, moving eastwards by about four metres since 1980. We can only speculate what the long-term effect of this will be.
- The sheer scale of global emissions and consequent global warming has also caused the troposphere – the atmospheric layer where humans live and where greenhouse gases are trapped – to expand, and the stratosphere – which extends from about 20km to 60km above the Earth's surface – to shrink by 400 metres since the 1980s.

Scientists are calling for urgent international action and warning that to 'err on the side of danger is not a responsible action'.

The observable impacts of climate change include:

- Sea levels have risen by eight-nine inches (21-24cm) since 1880, rising by 3.4 inches since 1993. Flooding is just one of the challenges the world is already facing and one that more areas will face in the future as sea levels rise. Erosion of beaches and coastal lands, salinisation of soil and farmlands and saltwater intrusion into aquifers used for drinking water are happening now and are problems which will grow in the future. Natural systems may not be able to keep up with the rapid rates of sea level rise now being projected. The salinity of freshwater rivers and wetlands may increase. Tidal wetlands and mangroves, which have some ability to migrate in response to rising seas, may have nowhere to migrate to because of human development that hems them in.
- Plant and animal habitats have shifted as species expand into newly favourable areas and decline in increasingly hostile ones; trees are flowering earlier.
- New patterns of pests and diseases are emerging, affecting plants, animals and humans. For instance, the West Nile virus, dengue and malaria are borne by disease carriers such as mosquitoes. Mosquito habitats, reproduction and survival are dependent on climatic conditions such as temperature, fluctuation in rainfall, flooding, drought and humidity. As these change, mosquitoes become more prevalent in new areas, as do the diseases they carry. The West Nile virus has circulated in Africa since 1937, and up until the early 1990s human outbreaks were only reported in Africa and the state of Israel. Since then, new strains have appeared in Europe. A first appearance in the western hemisphere occurred in New York City in 1999, then in Argentina by 2005. Hence West Nile fever disease is increasingly found in areas where it has never been seen before.
- There are already increasing numbers of intense rainfall events. The wettest autumn in England and Wales since records began in 1766 occurred in October-November 2000, damaged nearly 10,000 properties and cost an estimated £1.3bn. A 2013 study showed that

'increases in greenhouse gases have contributed to the observed intensification of heavy precipitation events found over [the] Northern Hemisphere'. All climate models generally agree that precipitation will become more intense, and almost the entire world is expected to see a 16-24% increase in extreme, heavy precipitation intensity by 2100 as it warms.

Flooding, Britain, October 2021

- The intensity, frequency and duration of hurricanes, as well as the frequency of the strongest (Category 4 and 5) hurricanes, have all increased since the 1980s. Climate models project that while the total number of tropical cyclones (tropical storms, hurricanes, and typhoons) will remain the same or decrease, the proportion of severe Category 4 and 5 cyclones, with more damaging wind speeds, higher storm surges, and more extreme rainfall, will increase. The latitudes of highest intensity are also moving towards the North and South Poles. Increases in the intensity of heavy precipitation, due to increased atmospheric water content and risen sea levels, will amplify the flooding triggered by these cyclones.
- In contrast, drought conditions are now endemic across the west of North America and the western coast of South America. In Chile, a 15-year-long 'megadrought' threatens the future of its agriculture. In Central America the consequent agricultural destruction has driven mass migration to the north. There are more frequent and intense droughts expected across much of Europe – particularly in Mediterranean countries. Another extreme event in Europe in summer 2018 persisted

to the subsequent year 2019, a 'consecutive summer drought' which was unprecedented in 250 years.

Dried up river bed, Atacama Desert, Chile

- There have been more frequent, more intense and longer heatwaves. Since 1950 the number of record high temperature events has been increasing, while the number of record low temperature events has been decreasing. In summer 2003, a rare heatwave killed 15,000 people in France, and over 70,000 in total in Europe, one of the hottest summers across central and western Europe since 1500 CE. The Global Burden of Diseases, Injuries, and Risk Factors Study, the first comprehensive analysis of the global cause-specific temperature-attributable burden of deaths published in August 2021 in *The Lancet*, estimated 356,000 deaths linked to extreme heat in 2019. Unprecedented heat-waves in early 2022 in areas as far apart as India, Pakistan, the Horn of Africa and South America compounded the pre-existing crisis in world food production.

The extent of climate change effects on individual regions will vary over time as will the ability of different countries to mitigate or adapt to these changes due to the global inequality imposed by imperialist exploitation. The droughts, flooding and heatwaves will have severe economic effects on agriculture, leading to shortages of food and rising food prices as capitalists cash in. Disadvantaged and vulnerable populations, indigenous peoples, and communities dependent on agricultural or coastal livelihoods are already directly and disproportionately affected by climate change.

The reports from the IPCC were not the first scientific reports on climate change. ExxonMobil, one of the world's largest oil and gas companies, was aware of climate change as early as 1977, but spent decades refusing to publicly acknowledge it, and even promoted climate change denial. In July 1977, Exxon senior scientist James Black told executives, 'There is general scientific agreement that the most likely manner in which mankind is influencing the global climate is through carbon dioxide release from the burning of fossil fuels.'

The bourgeois media only made it an issue eleven years later following an appearance at the US Senate's Energy and Natural Resources Committee by James Hansen, former director of NASA's Institute for Space Studies, in June 1988. He explained that global warming was caused by human exploitation of fossil fuels, and that greenhouse gas emissions [were] 'changing our climate now'. But in 1989, Exxon created 'think tanks' to question climate science and lobbied against the signing of the Kyoto Protocol in 1998. About half of all greenhouse gases currently in the atmosphere have been released since 1988.

As Fidel Castro observed at the Rio Earth Summit in 1992, 'An important biological species — humankind — is at risk of disappearing due to the rapid and progressive elimination of its natural habitat. We are becoming aware of this problem when it is almost too late to prevent it. It must be said that consumer societies are chiefly responsible for this appalling environmental destruction.'[10]

Earth Strike North of the River protest, Trafalgar Square, June 2021.
PHOTO CREDIT: Steve Eason

10 See Rock around the Blockade's pamphlet *Revolutionary Cuba: the Streets are Ours!* 3rd edition, 2021. For the full text of Castro's speech, see www.liberationnews.org/fidel-castros-prescient-warning-on-climate-change.

two

THE ENVIRONMENT AND WORLD SUMMITS

a legacy of failure

It has become increasingly evident that the November 2021 Glasgow COP26 conference achieved nothing, let alone offered a path forward for humanity in addressing global warming or environmental destruction. It proved to be no different to the succession of conferences that started with Rio in 1992: they have consistently produced solemn assurances and promises that have meant zero. The advanced capitalist countries have never made any concession to the plight of the underdeveloped countries already experiencing the brunt of the climate crisis. The $100bn a year promised at Copenhagen in 2009 to help mitigate the impact of climate change has yet to materialise 13 years later; of the $80bn provided in 2019 only $20bn was for adaptation projects. In contrast, the G20 advanced capitalist countries spent $3.3 trillion on subsidising their fossil fuel industries between 2015 and 2020.

South London FRFI Cop26? Cop Out! Protest, Peckham, November 2021

The UN Environment Programme report published in October 2021 estimated that by 2030 'governments' production plans and projections would lead to around 240% more coal, 57% more oil, and 71% more gas than would be necessary to limit global warming to 1.5°C', and that such plans mean that production would be 45% more than the level needed to achieve the weaker goal of 2°C. Yet the final COP26 declaration could not say anything specific even about reducing coal output – it could only talk of 'phasing down' such production, not phasing it out. Just four days after the end of the summit, US President Joe Biden announced a sale of drilling leases for oil and gas for more than 80 million acres in the Gulf of Mexico. This is a president who in his election campaign declared: 'No more drilling, including offshore. No ability for the oil industry to continue to drill, period, ends, number one.'

Rio Earth Summit 1992: capital against the world

The 1992 UN Conference on Climate and Development set the tone for all the subsequent conferences on global warming, summarised by the opinion of one US delegate that 'environment protection has replaced communism as the great threat to capitalism'. The strongest lobby then as now was that of capital – the giant monopolies and the imperialist governments that represent them. The US delegation itself was under strict orders from then-President George Bush to add qualifications such as 'where possible' or 'if appropriate' to agenda paragraphs that demanded any commitment by governments to change their national policies or the lifestyles of their people. The British government under Conservative Prime Minister John Major led the move to drop all references to the environmental responsibilities of multinational corporations. The European Community and Japan challenged the right of developing nations to restrict access to their timber resources. Each imperialist government was out to protect its own industries and to evade responsibility for environmental degradation.

The resulting treaty on climate change was originally to limit greenhouse gas emissions to their 1990 level by 2000. Given the damage that had already been created by 1990, this was hardly radical. But it was too much for the gigantic car and oil lobbies; the treaty was reduced to obliging signatories to come up with proposals to limit emissions. There was no Treaty on Forest Protection; it was replaced by a non-binding declaration of principles which environmentalists denounced as a 'Chainsaw Charter'. A Biodiversity Treaty was agreed (without US signature) which was supposed to be about the protection of plant and animal life, but instead talked about compensation for nations whose resources were exploited or destroyed, omitting to set out any mechanism to enforce this. Above all, there were no binding commitments on multinationals or imperialist governments, nothing that might interfere with the pursuit of profit. No cuts in air pollution, no halt to toxic waste dumping, no change to the unfair trade terms and debt repayments that force environmental destruction onto the poorer nations.

Fidel Castro at the Earth Summit, Rio, 1992

It was left to Cuba's socialist president, Fidel Castro, in his speech to the Summit[11] to expose the two systemic reasons for the climate emergency: the gross, unequal consumption necessary to sustain wealthy capitalist

11 See footnote 10.

countries, and the flagrant economically-motivated attacks on oppressed and poorer countries. The impoverishment, economic underdevelopment and indebtedness, and the pollution and devastation of their lands and waters are the direct consequence of the rapacious enrichment of the wealthy.

In 1992 Castro judged this situation had gone almost too far to be solved. Only by establishing a 'just international economic order', meaning cooperating fairly to advance all societies equally, could humanity be saved.

The Kyoto Protocol

Years of negotiation followed the Rio Summit to produce an agreement on containing carbon emissions which was agreed at the 1997 conference in Kyoto, although the US administration refused to ratify it. The Kyoto Protocol required the advanced capitalist countries to reduce emissions by 5.2% compared to 1990 levels. However, it did not come into force until 2005. Emissions soared by 40% between 1990 and 2009. Kyoto also introduced the concept of carbon offsetting, creating the carbon markets which amount to pollution-by-permit and in essence allow imperialist countries to dump carbon in the poorer countries.

In the year that Kyoto came into force, Britain's Labour Prime Minister Tony Blair warned the Davos World Economic Forum that governments could not be expected to push through changes that would seriously damage their economic prospects: 'If we put forward as a solution to climate change something that involves serious cuts in growth or standards of living – it matters not how justified it is – it simply won't be agreed to.' Such are the true limits to climate control under capitalism.

The battle at Copenhagen

The war between the imperialist countries and the underdeveloped world exploded into the open at the COP15 conference in Copenhagen in 2009. The then Labour government worked with the US to push through an agenda which ignored the demands of the poorer countries. The Africa

Group of countries had demanded $400bn a year to finance measures to contain climate change; Britain and the US co-opted Ethiopia and Bangladesh as token poor countries into a select group of 25, ignoring more than 160 other nations. The Ethiopian prime minister agreed to a mere $100bn annual finance from the imperialist countries between 2010-2012, while US President Barack Obama rejected even the pitiful emission cuts offered by the imperialists, well below the 40% by 2020 demanded by both scientists and the poorer nations at that time.

To add insult to injury, Obama preferred to make a stand on verification of emission cuts by the poorer countries; the Sudanese chair of the G77 group of underdeveloped countries said Obama had 'asked Africa to sign a suicide pact, an incineration pact, in order to maintain the economic dominance of a few countries'. Cuba, Bolivia and Venezuela denounced what was happening; Bolivian President Evo Morales saying 'The budget of the US is $687bn for defence. And for climate change, to save life, to save humanity, they only put up $10bn.'

Leaders from Nicaragua, Cuba, Bolivia, Ecuador and Venezuela greet the crowd at the Cochabamba People's Summit, Bolivia April 2010

In response, the Bolivarian Alliance for the Americas convened a World People's Conference on Climate Change in Bolivia in April 2010. The resulting Cochabamba Agreement recognised that: 'The capitalist system has imposed on us a logic of competition, progress and limitless growth. This regime of production and consumption seeks profit without limits, separating human beings from nature and imposing a logic of domination upon nature, transforming everything into commodities: water, earth, the human genome, ancestral cultures, biodiversity, justice, ethics, the rights of peoples, and life itself.'

Calling for the establishment of an International Climate and Environmental Justice Tribunal 'that has the legal capacity to prevent, judge and penalise states, industries and people that by commission or omission contaminate and provoke climate change', the Agreement also demanded that developed countries:

- commit to reducing carbon emissions by at least 50% based on 1990 levels, eliminating carbon markets and other offset mechanisms;
- recognise, support and give full rights to climate migrants;
- establish a climate fund of 6% of their annual GDP created to honour climate debt run up in the destruction of natural environment, seas and contaminated air space.

The Agreement was a challenge to the failure of the Copenhagen Summit (COP15), and asserted an anti-capitalist message against the prevarication of the developed countries. It declared unequivocally: 'Humanity confronts a great dilemma: to continue on the path of capitalism, depredation, and death, or to choose the path of harmony with nature and respect for life.'

The clarity of the anti-capitalist standpoint of the Cochabamba Agreement, its unapologetic expression of the primacy of the interests of the poorest nations and their peoples, the real content it gives to the notion of climate justice, makes it essential to the political standpoint of a serious climate change movement.[12]

12 Sam McGill, 'Ecosocialism or imperialist destruction', FRFI 215 June/July 2010.

Earth Strike North of the River and FRFI rolling picket of Oxford Street, January 2020. PHOTO CREDIT: **Steve Eason**

Paris 2015: spiralling towards disaster

By the time of the Paris COP21 conference in December 2015, carbon emissions had spiralled upwards from 23 billion tonnes in 1990 to 31.3 billion tonnes in 2014; 2015 was set to be the hottest year on record. In 2013, fossil fuel subsidies totalled £550bn, more than four times those for renewable energy.

In the lead-up to the conference, *Le Monde Diplomatique* reported that 'the overall target for reductions, the definition of the global emissions peak and the monitoring mechanisms are still very vague. Taxing sea and air travel remain taboo. And the re-evaluation of a mode of production that is pushing humanity towards crisis has been postponed.'

Draconian state of emergency laws banned protests at the conference, and dozens of climate activists were placed under house arrest. The declared aim of the conference was to hold the increase in global average temperature to well below 2°C above pre-industrial levels and to ensure that efforts are pursued to limit the temperature increase to 1.5°C. It once again committed to finding $100bn in public and private money to finance climate mitigation projects in the under-developed countries.

No extra clarity came with the conference itself, and the resulting agreement was anyway non-binding. Alberto Saldamando, a lawyer involved with the Indigenous Environmental Network, laid the deal bare:

'The Paris accord is a trade agreement, nothing more. It promises to privatise, commodify and sell forested lands as carbon offsets in fraudulent schemes. These offset schemes provide a financial laundering mechanism for developed countries to launder their carbon pollution on the backs of the global south. For example, the United States' climate change plan includes 250 million megatons to be absorbed by oceans and forest offset markets. Essentially, those responsible for the climate crisis not only get to buy their way out of compliance but they also get to profit from it.'

Nottingham FRFI present a 'Race to Disaster' award to Barclays Bank during their protest which highlighted the role of British banking on the environment, November 2021

Bolivian President Evo Morales was one of the few voices to address this reality in Paris. Delivering a manifesto 'to save Mother Earth and life', he said: 'Capitalism has fostered, introduced and driven the most savage and destructive formula against our species'.

In 2020, the Trump administration pulled the US out of the Paris Agreement on the grounds of protecting the US economy. Britain, the EU and Norwegian contravention has been less well documented: Britain by expanding fracking domestically, Norway by continuing Arctic oil exploration and Germany by tearing down Hambach Forest to access huge coal deposits underneath.

Since the 2015 Paris Agreement, the 60 largest private banks have invested \$3.8 trillion in fossil fuels; the big five British banks (Barclays, HSBC, Lloyds, NatWest and Standard Chartered) invested \$190bn between 2018 and 2020. In May 2021, a mere 14% of Barclays' shareholders backed a resolution calling on the bank to align its fossil fuel investment policy with that required by the Paris trajectories. The influence of summits and conferences over the past 30 years shows no effect on carbon emissions.[13]

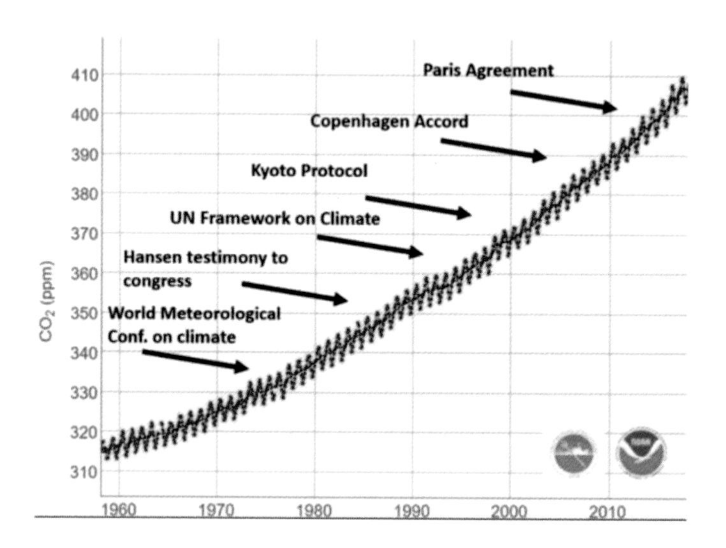

British presidency of COP26

In the lead-up to COP26, the Royal Institute of International Affairs issued its own Climate Change Risk Assessment 2021 for heads of government. This had three key points:

- The world is dangerously off track to meet the Paris Agreement goals.
- The risks are compounding.
- Without immediate action the impacts will be devastating in the coming decades.

The report said that there is a 10% chance of global temperatures rising by 7°C. A failure to slash emissions by 2030 will mean that 3.9 billion people

13 Graph from South East Climate Alliance, 1 February 2021, www.seclimatealliance.uk

will be hit by major heatwaves at various intervals of time; 400 million people will be exposed to temperatures that exceed 'the workability threshold', and the number of people on the planet exposed to heat stress exceeding the survivability threshold is likely to surpass 10 million a year. The report dismissed what it calls a 'fad' of making net zero carbon emissions pledges which have no meaning, and pointed out that croplands hit by severe drought will rise by 32% per year by 2040 without drastic action now.

The month before COP26, British Prime Minister Boris Johnson pledged to make the City of London 'the global centre of green finance'. This 'greenwashing' conceals the role the City of London plays in managing the flows of capital for some of the world's largest oil, mining and food multinationals. A recent study conducted by Greenpeace using the UK government's metrics for carbon emissions estimated that the amount of CO_2 production through projects financed by Britain's banks and asset managers around the world is nearly double the country's domestic annual carbon emissions. When the Environment Act was passed by the House of Commons on 26 March 2021, the regulations requiring companies to 'root out links to illegal deforestation from their supply chains' did not extend to the banks, which invested £900m in deforestation ventures in 2020.

The conflict between the imperialist and the underdeveloped countries was less apparent at COP26, mainly because it proved immensely difficult for indigenous communities and underdeveloped countries to send delegations, because of the Covid-19 pandemic and resultant high costs. They arrived in Glasgow to be outnumbered two to one by lobbyists for fossil fuel companies registered as part of country, NGO or direct corporate delegations. The sponsors' list for COP26 included Unilever and Reckitt as 'principal partners'. Paul Polsen, Unilever CEO from 2009 to 2019, was a 'friend of COP'. Unilever's products include those based on exploitative palm oil plantations in West Papua and Nigeria. US President Joe Biden turned up without any plans for reducing emissions because the US Congress had not approved them.

Unilever

Unilever is a British multinational headquartered in London. It is the world's third largest consumer goods company, with brands from Hellman's to Domestos, PG Tips to Marmite, selling over 400 brands in over 190 countries to 2.5 billion people. The firm grew up with the British Empire; as Lever Brothers it pioneered mass advertising, starting with Sunlight soap in 1885. Soap needed palm oil, and founder William Lever bought African land for the equivalent of a few bags of salt to develop palm oil plantations; in the Congo Lever plantations employed forced labour overseen by Belgian King Leopold II's brutal colonial forces. Lever subsequently controlled land equivalent to half the size of England in the Congo; he wrote 'The land of the world in any part of the world, ought to be in possession of those who can develop it and its resources…' When Unilever left the Democratic Republic of Congo in 2009 it owed wages worth $45m, which have still not been paid and which the workers' union is still pursuing through the Organisation of Economic Development. Unilever makes $45m every six and half hours of every day.

Earth Strike North of the River protest outside Unilever, July 2020.
PHOTO CREDIT: **Steve Eason**

In the opening session Johnson spoke with distracting metaphors of football, fillms and the nuclear 'doomsday clock'. However, the most influential member within the British COP26 presidency was not an environmentalist but Mark Carney, a former governor of both the Bank of England and the Bank of Canada. Given the dual role of UN Special Envoy for Climate Action and Finance as well as being the Prime Minister's own finance adviser for the conference, Carney was entrusted by the UN, Britain and the capitalist world to ensure their interests dominated COP26. Carney is also the Vice Chair of Brookfield Asset Management. This private firm handles investments of $625bn, which means his commitment to finance capital long pre-dates and far outweighs his entrusted brief for 'climate action'. In the end the conference proved unwilling even to press for an end date for coal extraction, and the phasing out of coal and fossil fuel subsidies was critically weakened.

The exclusion of the big polluters – the armed forces

The military forces of the imperialist powers function as the long arm of their national interests. Their troops are sent to dominate countries that dare to claim sovereignty over their own natural resources. These armed forces are also some of the biggest consumers of fossil fuels. 'The world's militaries combined, and the industries that provide their equipment, are estimated to create 6% of all global emissions', according to Scientists for Global Responsibility (SGR).[14] However, countries do not have to include military emissions in their targets or report them to the United Nations.

The biggest offender in this regard is the US military. Were it a country, 'its fuel usage alone would make it the 47th largest emitter of greenhouse gases in the world, sitting between Peru and Portugal. In 2017, the US military bought about 269,230 barrels of oil a day and emitted more than 25,000 kilotons of carbon dioxide by burning those fuels. The US Air Force purchased $4.9bn worth of fuel, and its navy $2.8bn, followed by the army at $947m and the

14 Stuart Parkinson, 'The carbon boot-print of the military', *Responsible Science* 2, January 2020.

marines at US$36m.'[15] The SGR study estimates that the British military emits 11 million tonnes annually of carbon dioxide equivalent – equal to the emissions of six million average cars.

Newcastle FRFI, November 2021

Given the central importance of their armies to upholding the world order which works in their favour, it is unsurprising that the rich nations ignore or downplay the significance of the military when calculating adherence to emissions targets such as those set by the Paris Agreement. Within the military, climate change is viewed only as a 'threat multiplier' that will make operations more volatile but not alter their fundamental purpose. The 2021 UK Strategic Defence Review identified climate change as a 'major security threat'. In early 2021, *The Times* reported that the Royal Navy was sending a frigate to the

15 Benjamin Neimark, Oliver Belcher and Patrick Bigger, 'US military is a bigger polluter than as many as 140 countries – shrinking this war machine is a must', *The Conversation*, 24 June 2019.

Arctic Circle to counter the perceived 'Russian strategic advantage over trade routes' opened up by the melting ice caps. The priorities of British imperialism are clear.[16 17]

The Swedish environmental activist Greta Thunberg was right in September 2021 to dismiss the words of politicians like Johnson as so much 'blah, blah, blah' saying 'Build back better. Blah, blah, blah. Green economy. Blah blah blah. Net zero by 2050. Blah, blah, blah. This is all we hear from our so-called leaders. Words that sound great but so far have not led to action. Our hopes and ambitions drown in their empty promises.'

FRFI, Earth Strike North of the River and Papua Militant International speaking at COP26 People's Summit, Glasgow, November 2021

It could not be anything else: a system driven by profit and directed by the interests of the major imperialist powers has to disguise its deeds with the empty, meaningless phrases of its hired politicians. To tell the truth about the climate crisis, let alone act on it, is an impossibility for capitalism.

16 Marc Bennetts, 'Warmer world lets Russian ship cross frozen Arctic on return from China', *The Times*, 23 February 2021.

17 Larisa Brown, 'Royal Navy to defend Arctic trade as ice melts', *The Times*, 10 March 2021.

three

IMPERIALISM and the environment

> 'Even an entire society, a nation, or all simultaneously existing societies taken together, are not owners of the earth. They are simply its possessors, its beneficiaries, and have to bequeath it in an improved state to succeeding generations.'[18]
> **Karl Marx**

How the intensification of production leads to imperialism

To understand imperialism is it is necessary to understand the history of capitalism – for it is capitalist relations of production that are the seed that grew into the global monster, imperialism.

The industrial revolution started in England towards the end of the 1700s. It transformed social conditions and class relations within decades. The profound and rapid changes to production methods and their impact on class structure were described and analysed not only in the works of Marx and Engels in the 19th century but also in the art and culture of the age. The following extract from Thomas Hardy's 1891 novel *Tess of the D'Urbervilles*, depicts rural, landless workers labouring under the conditions of capitalist agri-business.

> *'It is threshing day at Flintcomb-Ash, and all the women gather around the sinister red threshing-machine. Nearby is a black, smoking engine, tended to by an engineer who serves its fire and industry and looks out of place in nature. He is strange and Northern and seems like a servant of Hell. The women start to work, feeding the ravenous machine with*

18 Karl Marx, *Capital: A Critique of Political Economy,* Volume 3, Penguin Edition, 1981, p911.

> *corn. Old men talk of the hand-labour of the old days, which got better results. Tess does not even have time to talk, she must work so fast to satisfy the machine'.*[19]

This band of women harvesters travels the countryside in search of work. For over a hundred years the steady enclosures of common land and the clearances of rural communities had destroyed the English peasantry as a class and reduced them to wage workers in both town and country. The new, mechanised methods of production were the property of the private landlord and factory owners, intensifying the exploitation of the working class for the owners with ruthless efficiency.

These are the social, economic and human conditions that grew into imperialism, the highest stage of capitalism, today exporting capital to every corner of the globe in the search for investment opportunities and super-profits. The Kenyan novelist and playwright, Ngũgĩ WaThiong'o captures the impact of this economic system on the lives of workers of the colonised nations labouring in the service of imperialism. Like Tess, their lives are dominated by the machine. In the play *I Will Marry When I Want*, the factory worker, Gĩaamba, describes his existence.

> *'Look at me. It's Sunday. I'm on my way to the factory. This company has become my God. That's how we live. You wake up before dawn. Before you have drunk a cup of milk-less tea. The Siren cries out. You dash out. Another Siren. You jump to the machine. You sweat and sweat and sweat. Another Siren. It's lunch break. You find a corner with your plain grains of maize. But before you have had two mouthfuls. Another Siren. The lunch break is over. Go back to the machine. You sweat and sweat and sweat. Siren. You meet your wife returning from the fields. Bye, bye. You tell her as you run to the machine. Here, take this. Two hundred shillings. The rest to Europe. By that time, you have sold away your body...your blood... your wife. Even your children! Why, because you hardly ever see them!'*[20]

19 Thomas Hardy, *Tess of the d'Urbervilles*, 1891.
20 Ngũgĩ WaThiong'o, *I Will Marry When I Want*, 1982.

Forty years on from Ngũgĩ's writings these conditions of exploitation have intensified further and deeper around the globe. Millions more sweated wage workers labour for the imperialist companies that are robbing and pillaging their lands.

This is imperialism

Under the capitalist system human labour and the natural world are exploited in the insatiable drive for profits that underpins the never-ending process of capital accumulation. Free competition turns into monopoly: ownership and control become increasingly concentrated into a few hands. Capital spreads across national boundaries to find new sources for exploitation, expanding into an international system where advanced capitalist countries loot and plunder wealth from every continent on Earth. This is imperialism. While most of the underdeveloped world is now formally independent, imperialist countries such as Britain exert neo-colonial domination through ownership and control of the world's resources, markets and finances. This control is exercised by:

Earth Strike North of the River protest outside Unilever, July 2020.
PHOTO CEDIT: Steve Eason

- monopoly companies and banks hosted in the imperialist countries;
- international financial institutions like the World Bank and IMF;
- and the imposition of unpayable debt on the developing world.

The result is a dependent development that serves the needs of the imperialist economies. This also prevents the dependent countries' resources being used to meet the needs of their people, the majority of the world's population.

Meanwhile, rivalries between imperialist powers lead to investment and trade wars and military interventions in dependent nations. In recent decades, as the underlying economic crisis has deepened, this has resulted in extensive destruction of countries in the Middle East and North Africa, costing millions of lives, triggering mass migration and displacement and further impoverishing the regions' people.

Which are the top carbon polluters?

A 2015 report on historical greenhouse gas emissions from 1850 until 2012 showed that the US was responsible for 20.2% of such emissions, the European Union (including Britain) 17.3%, and China 12.1% of total cumulative global emissions. Britain accounted for 22% of the EU's CO_2 emissions. On a per capita basis, Britain is the world's top carbon dioxide emitter and has made the largest historical contribution to global warming, followed closely by the US. China, currently the world's leading emitter, is in 19th position for historical emissions.

Mining and other extractive monopolies along with agribusiness multinationals dominate world production. 100 companies have been responsible for about 71% of the world's greenhouse gas emissions since 1988, with more than half of emissions linked to just 25 companies including British and US oil giants Shell, ExxonMobil, BP and Chevron. Their activities emit vast quantities of greenhouse gases, pollute water, air and land and displace whole communities, turning some into wage workers on a minimal wage and driving others to become stateless migrants. Examples of such companies are:

- **Anglo American**, one of the world's largest mining companies, with revenues of $4.1bn in 2017, and which operates eight mines, mainly copper or nickel, in Peru, Chile, Colombia and Brazil. It is the world's biggest producer of platinum, with about 40% of world output. Anglo American also owns 85% of the diamond monopoly De Beers. It has a network of subsidiary properties including mines, estates, farms, ships, planes, a police force and an intelligence system.

- **Glencore**, the Anglo-Swiss multinational which is the world's fourth biggest mining company, had annual revenues of $203.8bn in 2021, more than three times those of BHP ($60.8bn in 2021). Glencore sends Congolese children down mines for cobalt at the equivalent of £1.25 a day. Cobalt is needed for electric cars, laptops and mobile phones; Tesla, Apple, Microsoft and Samsung drip with blood and dirt, courtesy of Glencore. The company operates in some 50 countries, including in a string of tax havens, across six continents. Glencore's mines use up to 100 million litres of clean drinking water a day, but dump toxic, heavy metal-laden effluent into rivers, such as the Sali Dulce river basin in Argentina, and river Calenturitas in Colombia. Argentinean and Peruvian police have violently attacked demonstrators protesting against the mines with live ammunition, rubber bullets, tear gas and dogs, using stress positions, and racist abuse.

Earth Strike North of the River protest outside Glencore, February 2020

- **BHP Billiton**, the largest multinational mining firm in the world by market capitalisation, is Anglo-Australian, and made $13.5bn profit in 2021. BHP operates five mostly copper mines in Chile, Peru, Brazil and Colombia. Brazil's worst-ever environmental disaster occurred in November 2015 when the Fundao dam to hold tailings waste at the Samarco mine (a joint venture between Brazilian-owned mining company Vale and BHP) collapsed, killing 19 people.
- **Royal Dutch Shell**, a British oil and gas multinational now operating as Shell plc, has operated in Nigeria since the discovery of oil between 1956 and 1965 in Ogoniland, in the eastern Niger Delta. There have been frequent oil spills in the region, 550 in one year alone, leaving behind devastated natural vegetation which included a dense mangrove forest that formed a self-sustaining coastal defence against Atlantic storms.
- **ExxonMobil** was formed in 1999 from the merger of Exxon (formerly Standard Oil of New Jersey) and Mobil (Standard Oil of New York). It is known in Britain for Esso and Mobil petroleum. In 2019 ExxonMobil filed a lawsuit against the Cuban state-owned oil company Cuba-Petroleo and Cuba Export-Import Corporation, CIMEX, over the expropriation of a refinery, petrol stations and other property in 1960 by the revolutionary government. This attack on socialist Cuba is facilitated by Title III of the US 'Cuban Liberty and Democratic Solidarity' (LIBERTAD) Act of 1996 (Helms-Burton Act). ExxonMobil demands $280m from Cuba.

FRFI protest against ExxonMobil's attacks on socialist Cuba, Central London, October 2019

These huge multinational entities operate through hundreds of subsidiaries, zombie or shell companies and state-held assets such as the South African Public Investment Corporation, Qatar Holdings, Vedanta Resources and Konkola Copper Mines, to name but a few. Finance flows through financial institutions like Barclays Bank, BlackRock and others, including hedge funds and of course shareholders which include the pension board of the Church of England and local councils.

Earth Strike North of the River protest outside BlackRock, September 2020. Protestors highlighted the destructive impact of BlackRock's mining interests in West Papua. PHOTO CREDIT: **Steve Eason**

The intensification of agricultural production has enormous costs for the planet and has reached the limits of what is possible. Yields of the world's four main crops which provide the staple diet of most of the world's population – corn, rice, wheat and soybeans – are stagnating. Extreme climate-related disasters doubled in number between 1990 and 2016, harming both productivity and output.

Capitalist agriculture is not sustainable agriculture. To obtain maximum growth, agribusiness uses a variety of technologies:

Genetic monoculture

To ensure predictability, new plants in plantations are propagated by taking cuttings. Part of the plant, often a piece of root, is cut off and used to grow genetic clones, with the result that all the crop in each plantation is genetically identical. This genetic similarity means that each plant has an identical immune response to pathogens. Consequently, if a pathogen manages to overcome the immune system of one plant in a plantation it can overcome them all. The spread of disease is then facilitated as plants are packed into an unnatural density in huge plantations. A particular problem arises with diseases that begin with long asymptomatic periods because a cutting from an infected plant will grow into a mature plant that is also infected. New plantations are commonly infected from the start.

Artificial selection

The meat industry is also affected by this lack of genetic diversity. The livestock industry uses specially bred, ultra-productive animals. As a result, 75% of the world's food comes from just 12 plant species and five animal species. Natural selection, which in wild animals and plants allows immune systems evolution to track pathogens and ensure within-species variation, has been replaced with artificial selection. This does not allow an ecosystem to function correctly. Biodiverse areas contain numerous harmless pathogens that have been passed back and forth between animals over time. The co-evolution of pathogens and animals has led to a natural defence system that has historically evolved to keep large-scale disease outbreaks in check.

Genetically modified organisms (GMOs)

Another technology used to maintain the flow of profit is the use of genetic modification or genetic engineering as it is also called. This creates plants that are of higher yield, adaptable to periods of drought and more resistant to pests and diseases. The nutritional value of plants can be increased by adding particular vitamins, minerals and nutrients to a crop. Shelf-life can be increased and flavour and appearance can also be modified.[21] By 2020, more than 90% of US corn, upland cotton, and soybeans used genetically modified varieties. Most of these genetically modified seeds are herbicide

21 Chris Robert, 'Capitalism and the banana Crisis', FRFI 280 February/March 2021.

tolerant, insect resistant, or both and are specifically sold to farmers as allowing herbicide to be easily applied without harming crop yield. India has been a particular target as a massive testing ground for genetically modified crops by the biotechnology industry with devastating results for both the environment and the people who live there.[22]

The deliberate manipulation of genetic varieties has a profound impact for biodiversity across the planet. The unintended consequences of genetic modification have led to the escalation of chemical use with irreversible results. Combined with the intensification of planting and the pressure to produce a profit, the planet has entered a vicious cycle of irreversible poisoning.[23]

FRFI joins Extinction Rebellion protest, April 2022

Super weeds

With the widespread use of herbicide tolerant plants, herbicide chemicals are freely sprayed on the unwanted growth of weeds in the crop. These in turn become resilient and more and more herbicide is needed to kill them off and the problem amplifies. As a result, in the US alone herbicide use expanded by 239 million kg between 1996 and 2011, accompanying the

22 Neeva Shanit, 'Indian farmers commit suicide in GM wasteland', FRFI 226 April/May 2012.

23 For more on the dangers of synthetic pesticides/biocides and the 'vicious cycle' read Silent Spring by Rachel Carson, 1962.

increased use of herbicide tolerant crops. When the modern herbicides become ineffective then older, more toxic chemicals are used, such as 2,4-Dichlorophenoxyacetic acid (2,4-D) and dicamba. The former was a component of the Agent Orange defoliant used by US forces in Vietnam, and exposure to it has been linked to reproductive problems, Parkinson's disease, and an elevated risk of non-Hodgkin's lymphoma, a blood cancer, and sarcoma, a skin cancer. Exposure to dicamba has also been linked to higher cancer rates. Both of these chemicals are volatile, and drift into the natural environment, putting nearby communities at risk of exposure. In 2015, the WHO's International Agency for Research on Cancer classified 2,4-D and glyphosate as possible human carcinogens.[24] In the US, 2,4-D and glyphosate are combined in a formulation called Enlist Duo for application to genetically modified crops. Glyphosate-based weed killers are widely used by councils in Britain to maintain parks and pavements.

Superbugs

GMO cropping also leads to the development of superbugs. A 2013 meta-analysis of 77 studies across eight countries on five continents in *Nature Biotechnology* found that in 2005 only 1 out of 13 major pest species were resistant to typical pesticides, but that this had increased to 5 out of 13 by 2011. As a result, the use of pesticide rises, further exacerbating the problem, alongside increasing environmental harm.

Pandemics and land use

The Global Virome Project estimates that there are 1.6 million unknown viruses circulating in wild animals, 700,000 of which can infect humans. In fact, the majority of pathogens found in humans originate in other animals. This is the phenomenon of zoonosis. 60% of 400 emerging diseases since 1940 are zoonotic. Since 1940, intensive agriculture was associated with more than 25% of all infectious diseases that emerged in humans and more than half of all zoonoses.

24 Around the world toxic areas known as 'Superfund sites' have developed. These are areas where chemical pollutants have been dumped from factories and landfills for decades.

A study published in Nature in August 2020 assessed nearly 7,000 animal communities across six continents, finding that as human-dominated land use increases, the number of animals that harbour disease-causing agents also increases. As agribusinesses continue to expand across the planet, outbreaks of pandemics will continue across the globe with increasing frequency. In addition to the ongoing cholera and HIV pandemics, new viruses have emerged in recent decades with both pandemics and outbreaks of pandemic potential now more frequent: these include SARs (CoV1) in 2003, influenza (H1N1) in 2009, MERS (CoV) in 2012 and SARs (CoV2), the virus that caused the Covid-19 pandemic.

Students join the Global Climate Strike, US, September 2020

Forever chemicals

Forever chemicals are non-biodegradable and hence persist and accumulate in soil, water, air, wildlife and human bodies. Several large chemical multinationals such as US-owned DowDuPont and Japanese-owned Daikin are responsible for them, companies with horrific environmental records. DowDuPont, formed by the 2017 merger of Dow Chemical and DuPont, is notoriously criminal. Union Carbide (taken over by Dow Chemicals in 2001) was responsible for the world's worst industrial chemical disaster in Bhopal, India in 1984. The multinational left 40 tonnes of carbaryl pesticide in the ground. A toxic explosion in the Union Carbide pesticide plant resulted in an estimated 22,000 deaths and 200,000 people badly affected. The 'accident' was a result of prioritising profit over safety. The effects of the disaster remain today and Bhopal has high rates of birth defects and miscarriage rates that are seven times higher than the national average.

Earth Strike North of the River protest outside BlackRock, September 2020.
PHOTO CREDIT: Steve Eason

Teflon is well-known as the coating in non-stick cookware. DuPont discovered Teflon in 1938. The manufacture of Teflon uses a chemical called C8 – purchased from the conglomerate 3M. C8 is one of thousands of 'forever chemicals' known as PFAS (per- and polyfluoroalkyl substances) produced by many chemical companies and present in everything from food packaging to cosmetics and building materials. Between 1962 and 1984 DuPont discovered a series of serious illnesses in animals exposed to C8, and dangerous levels of C8 in drinking water, yet neither the government nor public were informed. In 1981, women were barred from working in the Teflon division after two of seven pregnant workers gave birth to children with birth defects. Despite this, by 2003 DuPont had dumped 1,250 tonnes of C8 into the Ohio River in the US. C8 exposure in humans is linked to a range of illnesses such as thyroid disease, and some cancers. Exposure is so widespread that C8 has been detected in new-borns, breast milk and umbilical cord blood in humans. The truth about the toxic impact of these 'forever chemicals' is criminally covered up by multinational companies and governments. An example is the role of Michael McCabe, a former US Environmental Protection Agency official and aide to President Biden, who led DuPont's defence of C8.

The global seed market

Genetically modified crops are inseparable from the privatisation of seeds. Farmer-managed seed systems support rich agro-biodiversity, adaptation to local conditions, and natural crop resilience against climate and economic shocks through an economy of gifting, trading and exchanging seeds between small-scale and communal farms. Agribusinesses buy up farms in underdeveloped countries and industrialise production, destroying this smallholder production and the related system of free exchange and sharing of seeds. Entering into the chain of capitalist production, farmers are no longer able to produce autonomously. They must now buy seeds and agrochemicals from the landowner in order to maximise yield and profit. Thus the distribution of seeds is controlled by a few giant monopolies. Just six multinationals currently control over two-thirds of the industrial seed market and, as these companies merge, the market is placed in fewer and fewer hands. For farmers, only a few industrial seed varieties become available. Moreover, patents of genetically modified seeds often prohibit the replanting of seeds harvested from the crop (utility patents in the US), so farmers must buy seeds to replant each crop cycle – effectively they must rent seeds.[25]

25 Abdul Vajid, 'India: farmers challenge "invincible" Modi government', FRFI 280 February/March 2021.

Biofuel

Another investment opportunity for multinational companies is the developing biofuel industry, estimated to be worth nearly $250bn by 2027. Biofuel is any fuel that is derived from biomass – that is, plant or algae material or animal waste. Biofuels are promoted as 'carbon neutral' and a source of renewable energy; they are supposedly environmentally friendly because the CO_2 emitted when burning them is no more than is absorbed by the plants used to make them. However, such a claim ignores the considerable CO_2 emission associated with planting, cultivating, harvesting, transporting and processing the crop to turn it into ethanol. Furthermore, in order to meet world demand for ethanol, millions of acres of rainforest in countries like Argentina and Brazil will have to be cleared to make way for crops.

Another devastating effect is due to the enormous amounts of fertilisers, herbicides and pesticides, whose residues are washed into rivers, lakes and seas. As Fidel Castro pointed out in May 2007: 'Transforming food into fuel is a monstrosity…regardless of official statements assuring us that this is not a choice between food and fuel, reality shows that this is exactly the alternative: either the land is used to produce food or to produce biofuels.' The idea of using food for fuel (while millions do not have enough to eat) as a response to oil shortages and climate change is indicative of capitalism, which cannot accept measures that put limits on growth of consumption.

World flower trade

The flower and decorative plants trade is largely dominated by the imperialist countries, Holland and the US in particular. However, land use for floristry has increased in the developing countries, particularly Kenya, Colombia, Ecuador and Ethiopia. The value of the export market of the developing countries has been put at $4bn a year. The real costs to production must include the loss of fertile land taken over by multinationals, as well as the vast amount of water needed for flower growing, and usually this comes at the expense of clean water available to communities.

Earth Strike North of the River protest outside Unilever, July 2020.
PHOTO CREDIT: **Steve Eason**

Agricultural produce must not only be grown but also processed, packaged and delivered to the market for sale. One of the major corporations in this supply chain is the British-based company Unilever. In 2019, the Unilever brand was valued at approximately $4.16bn. Unilever sells over 400 brands in over 190 countries. It has 155,000 employees and sells to 2.5 billion people. The firm grew up with the British Empire, pioneering mass retailing and advertising. Scouring the world for markets, Unilever imposes the consumer habits of the developed capitalist countries on the poor and underdeveloped peoples and nations.

Plastics pollution

The majority of Britain's plastic waste ends up in landfill or the ocean, and Britain is rapidly running out of landfill capacity. British companies have shipped more than 2.7 million tonnes of waste to China and Hong Kong since 2012. China has now banned imports of plastic waste and in 2019, Malaysia ordered the closure of factories processing or storing plastic waste, and announced the return of 3,000 tonnes of plastic waste to its countries of origin. Yet in the first seven months of 2020, Malaysia received over 33,000 tonnes of plastic waste from Britain alone, 81% more than in 2019.

Plastic packaging is designed with aesthetics in mind rather than the environment, and Britain gets through seven million disposable coffee cups a day – 2.5 billion a year. The British plastics industry alone employs 180,000 people, turning over £17bn a year. Fossil fuel companies like ExxonMobil and Shell have invested more than $186bn since 2010 in 318 new 'cracking' facilities that will produce the raw material for everyday plastics.

Alternative biodegradable plastics made from starch polymers are possible, but more expensive to produce and therefore of no interest to mass producers despite plastic's pernicious effects. Today people around the globe are drinking water contaminated by plastic particles, with the impact on human health unknown.[26] The average number of fibres found in each 500ml sample ranged from 4.8 in the US to 1.9 in Europe. Then there is the 'plastic dust' from the wear and tear of tyres – 63,000 tonnes of it in Britain each year – which contributes to the poor quality of air and up to 700,000 microfibres shed with each wash by clothes made from synthetic polymers. In addition, plastic waste is polluting the seas, killing off aquatic life and strangling creatures to death.

April 2022, The #breakfreefromplastic coalition highlight plastic pollution on Freedom Island, Philippines

26 World Health Organisation, 'Microplastics in drinking-water', 28 August 2019.

Soviet poster, 'Purity of the Seas!' 1973

'The "essence" of the freshwater fish is the water of a river. But the latter ceases to be the essence of the fish and so is no longer a suitable medium for existence as soon as the river is made to serve industry, as soon as it is polluted by dyes and other waste products and navigated by steamboats, or as soon as its water is diverted into canals where simple drainage can deprive fish of its medium of existence.'[27]

Karl Marx and Friedrich Engels

The land of this planet is the property of the few

The number of people suffering from hunger worldwide is currently estimated to be 1.02 billion: it is a criminal fact that the countries that are the most food insecure are selling off land in order to secure food for other countries, in what has been dubbed 'the great land grab'. Sudan has agreed that investors can export 70% of the produce that will be created through land grab deals – yet Sudan is the recipient of the largest food-aid operation in the world. In Kenya, the Qatari government has agreed to fund the building of a coastal port in exchange for a lease of 40,000 hectares of land – despite the fact that an estimated 30% of Kenyans currently suffer food shortages.[28] Following the 2008 financial crash,

27 Karl Marx and Friedrich Engels, *The German Ideology*, Lawrence & Wishart, London, 1965, p.55

28 Neeva Shanti, 'Corporate land grabs in Africa', FRFI 222 August/September 2011.

there was a rush by big business to buy land as a safe investment. The non-profit organisation GRAIN records nearly $300bn of investment by private equity firms between 2008 and 2019 in agriculture and farmland alone.[29] This was particularly concentrated in Africa, where just 56 funds are known to have invested a total of $105bn.

Occupation of land sites for political reasons

Some specific areas of land have geo-political significance for the dominant imperialist powers over and above their commercial value. Palestine is one. Zionist propagandists often credit the settler-colonialist Israeli state with 'making the desert bloom', but the scale of pollution and environmental destruction by the Zionist state of land, water and air across Palestine is immense. Appropriation and 'cleansing' of the land by the Zionist state amounted to the destruction of over 700,000 olive and orange trees, and today native woodland containing indigenous species of trees accounts for a mere 10% of forested areas.

Placards from FRFI Stop Environmental Destruction in Palestine protest, November 2021

The Palestinian enclaves (post-1967) have increasingly been both host to polluting Israeli factories and used as dumping grounds for the Zionist state's waste and sewage. The B'tselem human rights group in Jerusalem reported in 2017 that the Israeli state transfers various types of

29 GRAIN is a small international non-profit organisation, see www.grain.org

waste to the West Bank: sewage sludge, infectious medical waste, used oils, solvents, metals, electronic waste and batteries, to name but a few. All are urban and industrial byproducts Israel generates within the 1948 borders, and they are made up of a wide range of unwanted substances that pose a real threat to the people and natural resources in their vicinity. A manufacturer of pesticides and fertilisers in Kfar Sava, north of Tel Aviv, was forced by an Israeli court to close down 'because of its environmental effects on land, public health and agriculture.' It relocated to the West Bank, where 'waste from the factory has damaged the citrus trees and polluted the soil in the area, in addition to the potential damage to groundwater.' Israeli settlements within the West Bank, illegal under international law, have been found to 'discharge millions of cubic metres of wastewater into the West Bank every year', turning agricultural areas into 'wastewater swamps', destroying Palestinian olive trees.[30]

The IMF in Ukraine

On 31 March 2020, Ukraine under President Volodymyr Zelensky passed a law lifting the country's prohibition on land transactions. According to an October 2019 survey, 73% of Ukrainian citizens opposed the new law. Ending the moratorium was part of a series of policy reforms imposed by the International Monetary Fund as the condition for a $5bn loan package, enabling agribusinesses access to Ukraine's 32 million hectares of fertile land. The law is the latest in a string of economic reforms that have been implemented in the aftermath of the country's 2004 Orange Revolution and the 2014 coup which overthrew the Yanukovich government for its reluctance to sign the Free Trade and Association Agreement with the EU.

These two events were led by the Ukrainian elite and sponsored by imperialist nations desperate to exploit the land in Ukraine. Multinational agribusiness firms – such as Cargill, Bayer, and DowDuPont – are, as a result, already heavily involved in Ukraine. In addition, in 2021 Ukraine started to auction off exploration permits to develop its lithium

30 B'tselem, *Made in Israel: Exploiting Palestinian land for treatment of Israeli waste*, December 2017.

reserves; researchers have speculated that the country's eastern region holds close to 500,000 tons of lithium oxide, as well as copper, cobalt and nickel.[31] All are natural resources that play critical roles in renewable energy technology and therefore Ukraine continues to attract the interest of big business and governments.

'The profit curve should go up all the time. In English we say that you look for conditions that will ensure an ever-increasing rate of profit'.[32] These are the words of a character from Ngũgĩ's 1982 novel *Devil on the Cross* 'dedicated to all Kenyans struggling against the neo-colonial state of imperialism'. These are the conditions of imperialism that are leading to environmental destruction on a global scale.

Protestors at the Global Climate Strike, Durban, South Africa, October 2020

31 'Before Invasion, Ukraine's Lithium Wealth Was Drawing Global Attention', The New York Times, March 2022.

32 Ngũgĩ WaThiong'o, *Devil on the Cross*, 1982.

four

NO 'GREEN' SOLUTION within capitalism

While land has long been commercialised under capitalism and turned into a commodity, the economic crisis has greatly extended this process. The World Bank is forcing underdeveloped countries to create legal titles for common lands so they can be traded as commodities. In the Malaysian state of Sabah on the island of Borneo, this has been taken a step further: the local government has sold two million hectares of an entire forest ecosystem. The deal allows the private equity investors involved

> *'...to acquire commercial rights to the natural capital in Sabah's forest ecosystem. The revenue from the rights to ecosystem services, such as water provisioning, carbon sequestration, sustainable forestry, and biodiversity conservation, over the next century was estimated at some $80bn.'*[33]

30%, or $24bn, would go to the investors; there is a stipulation that the Sabah government could not withdraw from the agreement, while the prime investors could sell their rights to others without government consent. The development of carbon markets is another form of the monetisation of nature: perversely, carbon pollution becomes an asset which can be traded like any other commodity. It is claimed that putting a price on carbon creates market incentives for companies to move investment into less-polluting technologies. Economic growth can then go on forever as it can be rendered benign for the environment. Even though this approach has

33 John Bellamy Foster, 'The defence of nature: resisting the financialisation of the Earth', *Monthly Review* Vol 73, No 11, April 2022.

failed miserably – and, as a result, ecosystems are collapsing faster than ever – carbon markets and other 'green' market mechanisms continue to grow.

Carbon markets

Carbon markets were introduced by the 1997 Kyoto Protocol. In effect, such markets parcel up the atmosphere so that 'permits to pollute' can be bought and sold like any other commodity. Carbon permits are first issued free of charge by governments. A cap is then placed on the amount of carbon that companies are allowed to emit annually. However, as a cap on emissions would be a fetter on economic growth, the 'cap' set by governments is never realistic. Firstly, the most polluting industries actually receive the biggest allocation of carbon permits. In addition, if individual companies wish or need to exceed their quota of carbon permits, they can buy carbon permits from other companies that are willing to sell their excess – essentially, these become carbon allowances.

Furthermore, companies also have the option to 'offset' their carbon pollution by investing in so-called 'pollution reduction projects'. In this deal, the number of carbon credits earned by investing in a so-called 'pollution reduction project' is calculated on the basis of the reduction in emissions promised by that project.[34] In theory, one carbon 'offset' credit supposedly equals one tonne of carbon dioxide, or a comparable amount of other greenhouse gases, removed from the air. Buying into carbon 'offsets' allows companies to earn a higher number of carbon credits. The carbon market is expected to grow sharply in the coming years as heavy emitters have promised to negate pollution by acquiring more carbon offsets.

Mark Carney has said the global market for carbon offsets can be expected to grow to $100bn in the decade ahead. Far from being a tool to cut carbon emissions, carbon 'offsets' are in reality a deceitful mechanism that actually allows the continuation of global emissions of carbon. In 2020, globally, companies purchased more than 93 million carbon

34 For a case study of carbon offsetting projects in monoculture tree plantations, see Bjork Lind, 'Green capitalism in crisis', 25 June 2021, on www.frfi.org.uk

credits, equivalent to the pollution from 20 million cars in one year; a 33% increase from 2019.

In reality, the long-term consequences of carbon markets are increased greenhouse gas emissions alongside soaring corporate profits. It therefore comes as no surprise that corporations which have an interest in delaying climate change mitigation and in continuing to burn fossil fuels are big advocates of carbon trading.

Reforestation and conservation

Capitalist schemes to reduce net carbon emissions also promote reforestation. But even if reforestation contributed to balancing the CO_2 from deforestation, the total carbon stored in new trees is only a fraction of the carbon emitted. In any case, forests are losing their ability to absorb carbon as trees dry out from drought and higher temperatures and the damage caused by the run-off from industrial agriculture. A 2019 study shows the African tropical forest carbon sink in 'long term future decline' with the Amazonian sink 'weakening rapidly'. Their carbon absorption peaked in the 1990s when they absorbed 46 billion tonnes, 17% of CO_2 emissions. Post-2010, they absorbed about 25 billion tonnes, 6% of emissions that decade.

Reforestation and conservation projects are driving local inhabitants off their land with little or no compensation, and forcing them to into poverty. It is estimated that 20 million people have been driven off their lands in the name of land and wildlife conservation. Today we see the Maasai in Ngorongoro, Tanzania fighting for their land after 70% of their homeland has been taken for conservation and investment reasons.

NGOs – the 'soft' power of imperialism

The system of imperialist 'green finance' is propped up by the aid network of international state aid agencies, non-governmental organisations (NGOs) and charities. The World Wildlife Fund (WWF) is one of the largest conservation groups in the world. It operates globally, with field offices in over 40 countries. In 2019 a year-long BuzzFeed News investigation reported that the WWF funded, equipped and worked directly with paramilitary forces to enforce conservation in six countries in Asia and Africa.[35] The WWF was accused of numerous acts of violence against scores of people, including beatings, torture, sexual assault and murder.[36] This example illustrates that control of 'conservation' is not in the hands of local communities. As noted on the WTF WWF website[37] 'The fact that abuses are perpetrated by eco-guards, park rangers and poaching patrols, suggests it might be time to seriously rethink how we do conservation.'[38]

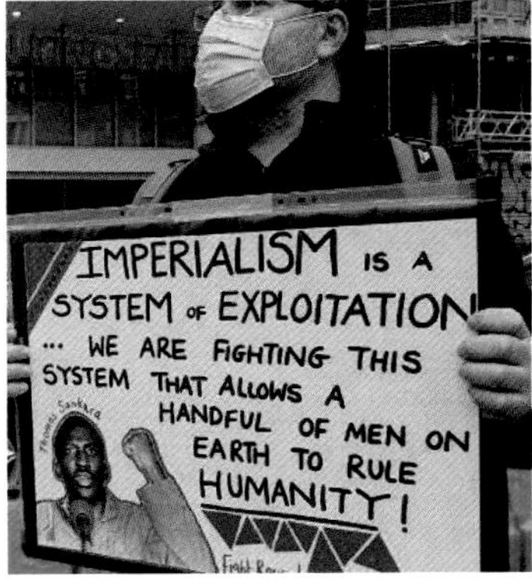

North and East London FRFI protest against imperialism, October 2021

This is not new. This is a continuation of the colonial occupation of the past, now in its imperialist stage. In the words of Thomas Sankara, the former revolutionary President of Burkina Faso;

'Imperialism is a system of exploitation that occurs not only in the brutal form of those who come with guns to conquer territory. Imperialism often occurs in more subtle forms, a loan, food aid, blackmail.'

Degrowth delusions

The project of sustainable capitalism is doomed from the start because maximising profit and saving the planet are mutually exclusive goals. Many environmentalists have come to recognise the relationship between economic growth and environmental degradation. However, in

35 Tom Warren and Katie J M Baker, 'WWF Funds Guards Who Have Tortured and Killed People', Buzzfeed News, 4 March 2019.

36 Survival International, WWF accused of deceit, cover-ups and dishonesty in US Congressional Committee hearing', 27 October 2021.

37 'WWF is complicit in the abuse and dispossession of Indigenous People', retrieved 8 July 2022 from www.wtfwwf.org

38 Sophie Grigg, 'When WWF's conservation looks like colonialism, it's time for a new approach', *The Independent*, 17 March 2019.

their defence of their class interests, some maintain that the fight for the environment does not mean a challenge to capitalism. Instead, they argue, a solution can be found within capitalism, by placing limits on national GDP growth.

The idea is that the capitalist economy can be slowed down, made to run at a 'steady state' or even to 'degrow'. The Degrowth Movement advocates economic stagnation to save the planet. However, it does not state who is going to pay the price for this stagnation. Degrowth under capitalism means economic recession – in reality this means poverty, austerity and war. It is undeniable that economic growth is the main driver of planetary ecological degradation, but capitalism is a system premised on it.

Tariq Fancy, a former chief of green investment at BlackRock, notes, 'I have looked inside the machine and I can tell you; business does not have this [capacity to grow sustainably]. It's not because they are evil, it's because the system is built to extract profits.'[39]

Earth Strike North of the River demonstration to Rio Tinto HQ, June 2021

A 'green' revolution will require more minerals

The World Bank predicted in a 2020 report that under a 2°C warming scenario (keeping average atmospheric temperature increases below 2°C in line with the 2015 Paris Climate Agreement), annual average global demand for 17 critical minerals would rise to a combined 3.1 billion tons from the current projection of 1.8 billion tons by 2050.[40] Demand for graphite, aluminium, cobalt and lithium would

39 Dominic Rushe, 'Green investing "is definitely not going to work"', says ex-BlackRock executive', *The Guardian*, 30 March 2021.

40 Reuters, World Bank, 'Minerals for Climate Action: The Mineral Intensity of the Clean Energy Transition', May 2020.

need to be ramped up 500% by 2050 to meet the growing requirement for 'clean energy' technologies. Ivan Glasenberg, then CEO of the world's largest mining firm Glencore, told the Qatar Economic Forum in June 2021 that copper supplies would have to increase by one million tonnes every year from its current 20-25 million tonnes per year to meet an expected annual demand of 60 million tonnes by 2050.[41]

According to a June 2019 report from SoS MinErals, if Britain were to meet its target of making all vehicle sales battery-electric by 2035, and replacing all UK-based cars and vans (excluding HGVs) with electric vehicles by 2050, it would need to 'produce':

- 207,900 tonnes of cobalt, just under twice the current total annual world cobalt production.
- At least 7,200 tonnes of neodymium and dysprosium which includes nearly the entire world production of neodymium.
- 264,600 tonnes of lithium carbonate, three quarters of the world's lithium production.
- 2.36 million tonnes of copper, almost 10% of the world's copper production.

Britain would also have to generate an extra 20% of electricity to charge all 31.5 million electric cars. Wind turbine or solar generation options for the added electrical power generation capacity would also have substantial extra demands for steel, aluminium, cement and glass as well as rare earth minerals.

British company Pensana Rare Earth has set up Saltend Chemicals Park, a rare earth facility in Yorkshire to process rare earths plundered from Angola's Longonjo mine. The facility will 'establish a sustainable supply chain for the manufacture of powerful permanent magnets critical for the offshore wind and electric vehicle industries in the UK and Europe'. In January 2021, Gerry Grimstone, British minister for investment, said: 'We very much welcome the proposal to establish a fully sustainable rare earth oxide magnet metal processing facility in the Humber region.' Another British company Rainbow

41 Copper supply needs to double by 2050, Glencore CEO says', Reuters, 22 June 2021.

Rare Earths, based in Guernsey, has expanded from Burundi into Zimbabwe and South Africa and could produce four thousand tonnes of neodymium and praseodymium annually, making Rainbow one of the largest producers in the world. Under the pressure of rich nations, debt and IMF policies, poorer nations have no choice but to 'trade' their rare earth resources at knock-down prices, so rich nations can go 'green'.

Brighton FRFI Rolling Picket Against the Climate Crisis, November 2021

The Green New Deal

To ensure capitalism's survival, its radical political representatives have called for a Green New Deal. The illusion that the Green New Deal is a serious political proposition comes from the term itself. It evokes US President Franklin Roosevelt's 'New Deal for the Forgotten Man' 1933-1939, a number of programmes focused on what were called 'the three Rs':

- Relief for the unemployed and poor;
- Recovery of the economy back to normal levels;
- Reform of the financial system to prevent a repeat depression.

State (federal) banks and agencies were set up to direct funding to increase industrial and agricultural production and expand employment.

The Green New Deal evokes this period of state intervention, but where Roosevelt was forced to subsidise the private sector with state funding to create jobs and work, the Green New Deal of today depends on the reverse: the transfer of booming private sector finance to fund a state sector which will then supposedly enable the transition from a carbon-heavy to a carbon-neutral economy. As US Congress representative Alexandria Ocasio-Cortez's chief of staff explained: 'There are literally trillions of dollars of private capital waiting to get invested in anything that is low risk with moderate returns. This is trillions of dollars that would flow into a Green New Deal.'[42]

Later 'left' versions of the Green New Deal also included universal health care, affordable and safe housing, and protections for workers' right to unionise, and were central to Senator Bernie Sanders's climate platform during the 2020 presidential primary. The Sunrise Movement, the largest North American climate-activist umbrella group, adds demands for Medicare for All and student-debt forgiveness. This, then, is a US 'leftist' platform for a reformist welfare statism. Its supporters ask how society can continue to pay for flooded subways, horrific droughts, deadly heat waves and uncontrollable wildfires but not be prepared to afford a Green New Deal.

In a further development, the Canadian writer and renowned environmental activist Naomi Klein established The Leap in 2015 as an organisation to promote:

> *'The belief that our overlapping crises of inequality and climate change stem from the same broken systems, and that we need intersectional solutions and alliances to rebuild our broken relationships to this planet and each other.'*

The Leap argues that the material aspirations of individuals and communities will have to change because the Earth has too few resources to offer every human a life of private opulence. What Earth can sustain, instead, are communal luxuries, more rapid-transit systems and cleaner air, for example.

This vision is however a utopian leap. It assumes that the raw materials, for 'clean' electricity, rare earth metals, lithium, and cobalt for batteries will replace coal, oil and carbonising fuels, but these raw materials are already extracted at great cost to the environment and communities in poorer nations

42 Max Ajl, *A People's Green New Deal*, Pluto Press, 2021, p84.

by ruthless capitalist firms which constantly intensify their rate of exploitation year by year. Asad Rehman from War on Want makes the point: 'In this new energy revolution, it is cobalt, lithium, silver and copper that will replace oil, gas and coal as the new frontline of our corporate destruction. The metals and minerals needed to build our wind turbines, our solar panels and electric batteries will be ripped out of the earth so that the UK continues to enjoy "lifeboat ethics": temporary sustainability to save us, but at the cost of the poor.'[43]

Only imperialist arrogance can ignore this inconvenient truth. It is a reality that is discounted in all New Green Deal proposals. Klein et al evade the obvious conclusion that it is not just capitalists but capitalism that has to be overthrown.

> 'Capitalist production...disturbs the metabolic interaction between man and the earth, i.e., prevents the return to the soil of its constituent elements consumed by man in the form of food and clothing; it therefore violates the conditions necessary to lasting fertility of the soil.... The social combination and organisation of the labour processes is turned into an organised mode of crushing out the workman's individual vitality, freedom and independence.... Moreover, all progress in capitalist agriculture is a progress in the art, not only of robbing the worker, but of robbing the soil; all progress in increasing the fertility of the soil for a given time is a progress towards ruining the more long-lasting sources of that fertility. The more a country starts its development on the foundation of modern industry, like the United States, for example, the more rapid is this process of destruction. Capitalist production, therefore, develops technology...only by sapping the original sources of all wealth—the soil and the worker.'[44]
>
> **Karl Marx**

43 Asad Rehman, 'The "green new deal" supported by Ocasio-Cortez and Corbyn is just a new form of colonialism', *The Independent,* 4 May 2019.

44 Karl Marx, *Capital: A Critique of Political Economy, Volume 1*, Penguin Edition, 1976, pp637-8.

FRFI placards, Extinction Rebellion demonstration, central London, November 2018

The Labour Party and the Green New Deal

The 2019 Labour Party election manifesto took up the same stance that state expenditure should be directed to overcome the challenge of climate change and ensure the wellbeing of society as a whole.

> *'[Labour will] launch a National Transformation Fund of £400bn and rewrite the Treasury's investment rules to guarantee that every penny spent is compatible with our climate and environmental targets. Of this, £250bn will directly fund the transition through a Green Transformation Fund dedicated to renewable and low-carbon energy and transport, biodiversity and environmental restoration'.*

Like Klein and others, the Manifesto said, 'The cost of not acting is far greater than the cost of acting', meaning that the devastation of climate change will wreak havoc on society. There is no plan to secure the cooperation of the huge financial hedge funds and banks that service the private sector. There is not the slightest recognition of the eco-destruction caused by British mining or oil multinationals, or the vast tracts of land that are being seized and then exhausted by unsustainable monoculture.

The truth is that there is no such thing as a 'green' solution within capitalism. A 'Green New Deal' is an advertiser's slogan, a confidence trick being perpetrated by those who believe there can be a capitalism without the capitalists. The reality in Britain is that the green sector of the economy is stagnant, as *The Guardian* reported:

> *'The Office for National Statistics (ONS) has this year reported that the "Green" sector in the UK has not grown since 2014. This includes employment in the manufacturing and construction industries in the low-carbon and renewable energy sector. The "net-zero" employment opportunities promised by the government are vanishing into hot air. The number of green businesses operating in the UK fell by over 13% in the last six years. The green agenda has not taken root and remains an illusion.'*[45]

Reject the Green New Deal – build real resistance

Billions of people across the planet are increasingly at risk from climate change. COP26 has not made the slightest difference. First there was denial, then there was the Green New Deal. There are no agreed plans, no written proposals, no steps to action, no analysis of costs and funding or responsibility to pay. In other words, the Green New Deal exists only as a wish list of the left and even this has increasingly been appropriated by sections of the establishment who pay lip-service to the need for 'green' policies. We have to reject the Green New Deal: it perpetuates the exploitative relationship that imperialist countries have with the underdeveloped world. We have to build real resistance to environmental destruction.

FRFI banner, Extinction Rebellion protest, London, April 2019

45 Richard Partington, 'UK green economy has failed to grow since 2014, according to official data', *The Guardian*, 17 February 2022.

five

ENVIRONMENTAL RESISTANCE IN BRITAIN

Over the past 30 years, there have been a number of environmental movements within Britain. A tradition of direct action that started with campaigns against road building projects in the 1990s continues today with the actions of Insulate Britain and Just Stop Oil. But alongside that there has been a different trend, one that has its roots in the reactionary position and habits of the traditional trade union movement and its left allies. This trend seeks at all times to maintain a petit bourgeois respectability, rejecting direct action in favour of dull demonstrations which just go from A to B and formal webinar-style meetings which block open discussions and from which progressive elements can be swiftly excluded.

Representative of this latter trend was the COP26 Coalition, established in 2021 to coordinate action on 'climate justice' during the COP26 conference, and describing itself as a 'UK-based civil society coalition of groups and individuals mobilising around climate justice during COP26. Coalition members include environment and development NGOs, trade unions, grassroots community campaigns, faith groups, youth groups, migrant and racial justice networks – to name a few.' Although its demands appeared to be broadly consistent with those of the Cochabamba Agreement, it avoided any direct critique of capitalism as the cause of the climate crisis. The Coalition's programme therefore represented a backward step compared to the Cochabamba Agreement, and was clearly geared towards attracting a layer of the population which may be alarmed at the impact of global warming but is determined not to give up its privileged lifestyle in order to confront the crisis – the middle classes or better off people in what the Coalition calls the 'Global North'.

Indeed, the programme went out of its way to soften everything that needed to be said. Euphemisms were deployed throughout its documents to ensure the minimum of clarity. The terms 'Global North' and 'Global South' were examples of this: the use of geographic terms was used deliberately to obscure what really matters: an economic relationship, one of exploitation, looting and plunder.

Calls to 'Rewire the system: Start the justice transition now' avoid any confrontation with the realities. What system? Evidently the authors were absolutely determined to avoid any use of the term 'capitalism', although the emotive language of 'injustices, poverty and inequalities' is everywhere. For the Coalition, what is required is 'a Worker-led Justice Transition shifting away from the fossil fuel industry and investing in renewable energy to create decent unionised "green" jobs and services.' But what does 'rewiring our system' mean? What actually needs 'rewiring'? What will that rewiring involve? Who will do it, and how? In the way it is presented, it seems to suggest an economic or technical solution – shift investment in fossil fuels to renewable energy, and somehow, we will address injustices, poverty and inequalities. In reality it is of course much more – but frightened as the Coalition is of the word 'capitalism', it is equally fearful of the word 'socialism' or even talking about state intervention. The Coalition belongs to a long tradition in Britain of cowardly 'socialists' – a trend which claims it cannot speak about socialism because it will scare off potential support when the truth is that its exponents have no real conviction that socialism is the answer to the problems that face humanity.

'We must cancel debts of Global South by all creditors', the Coalition declares. But how will 'we' do this, given that 'we' are not the creditors? In the context of a movement in Britain, it would need an all-out assault on the banks and the City of London. What force would lead the process? What politics would it need? It is as if the mere willing of such an end would be sufficient to achieve it, rather than the serious political struggle that it requires. It is the same with the Coalition's demand that there be a 'a fair share of effort from all countries' in tackling climate change, that the rich countries would have to provide 'grant-based climate finance'. Given that they have yet to cough up the $100bn a year they promised (mostly as loans) in 2009 at Copenhagen, how will this be achieved?

While the Coalition's programme does not specifically allude to a Green New Deal, the phrase 'decent green unionised jobs' is an oblique reference to it. The problem for the Coalition is that on the one hand something has to be said about green jobs to get the trade unions on board. On the other, highlighting policies associated with a Green New Deal risks alienating movements from poor countries that are fully aware that its achievement would depend on maintaining the existing exploitative relations between developed capitalist countries and their own nations. While the Coalition says that 'new infrastructures can't only be built in the Global North with resource extraction and human rights abuse in the Global South', these are the preconditions for such green jobs in the 'Global North'. And when that becomes a more specific call for a million such jobs in Britain, it is clear that its proposers have little regard as to the consequences for the plight of the exploited underdeveloped countries.

FRFI Glasgow at COP26 demonstrations, November 2021

The Coalition's programme failed to build a climate justice movement. Apart from the protest the Coalition organised in Glasgow on 6 November 2021, local demonstrations it called for on the 'Global Day of Action' were pitiful in size. They were led by the pillars of respectability which had formed the Coalition, a fictional 'broad coalition' to create equally fictional 'broad support' for a day of family fun and music, with carefully pre-selected speakers. Participation by younger people was notably absent. Rebranding itself as the Climate Justice Coalition will not alter this.

It was quite different from the 2019 school student strikes or even XR's programmes of direct action which had started in late 2018, and especially in stark contrast to the direct-action campaigns of the 1990s against the Twyford Down M3 extension, the M11 link road and the Newbury Bypass or the Youth Climate Swarm and Just Stop Oil actions of today.

Twyford Down

In 1989 the Conservative government published a White Paper entitled 'Roads for Prosperity' which set out plans to extend road networks by 24,000 miles, including an extension to the M3 at Twyford Down, and the construction of the Newbury bypass. Both projects resulted in widespread protests and opposition.

Direct Action at Twyford Down road protest, 1992

In Twyford an encampment was established in 1992 to occupy the land to prevent its excavation and block the path of construction equipment. However, they were violently evicted the following year by the construction companies' security force, G4S; in one episode, a protestor was strangled and left unconscious for half an hour on the Down while others were beaten, sometimes in full view of the press.

M11 link road campaign

The M11 link road was to be a four-mile stretch of motorway running through Leyton, Leytonstone and Wanstead in East London. Protests got seriously underway when a 250-year-old chestnut tree on the proposed motorway route was scheduled for felling in late 1993. Local residents surrounded it to prevent its removal; when fencing was put up to stop them assembling, they tore it down. It took hundreds of police ten hours to remove the demonstrators before the tree was finally felled. Campaigners then prevented construction workers from gaining access to houses which had been compulsorily purchased for subsequent demolition along the route of the motorway. Sit-ins, building site invasions and sabotage hindered construction; police and security staff had to patrol building sites at an estimated £500,000 per month. Protestors built tunnels to prevent demolitions. The last major obstacle to the motorway, a group of houses in Claremont Road, required hundreds more police –some in riot gear – to support bailiffs carrying out evictions prior to demolition. The link road is now one of the most congested roads in Britain; the campaign against its construction doubled its cost and contributed to a decision to shelve the M12 in north-east London.

The Battle of Newbury

The Battle of Newbury in 1996 was a pivotal moment for the anti-roads movement. The Newbury bypass plans were to fell 10,000 mature trees to make space for the new road. What transpired was a nearly two-year campaign of encampments on various sites along the route, meaning at each point bailiffs had to physically fight protesters to remove them from trees. The tactics of occupying trees and living in tunnels under the trees greatly slowed the clearance; the cost of the road skyrocketed, adding an extra £30m to what was supposed to be a £74m project. Although the battle was lost, it marked the end of the Tory government's 'Roads for Prosperity' programme as the cost had been so great.

Mobilisation by the state against the Newbury Bypass protesters, 1996

The response of the Tory government was repression: a Bill which eventually became the Criminal Justice and Public Order Act 1994, sections of which specifically targeted protesters, travellers, squatters and the illegal rave scene. Opposition to the Bill led to a broad protest alliance which saw a Brighton courthouse squatted, a mass rave in Trafalgar Square, large-scale politically organised land trespasses, an occupation of the roofs of Parliament and a stand-off with police in Hyde Park.

Reclaim the Streets

One development from anti-roads campaigns of the time was the establishment of Reclaim the Streets (RTS) which swiftly became targeted by the media and politicians for its anti-capitalist, direct action ethos. It organised party-like demonstrations on motorways and major highways. In September 1996, it linked up with the Liverpool Dockers who at the time were on a 28-month long strike. After joining a march through the city, RTS activists occupied the Customs House and gantries over the

Mersey docks and harbours office to be met with a police offensive. The unity of struggles presented a real challenge to the ruling class and led to undercover surveillance of RTS activists and others in similar environmental groups.

On World Climate Action Day 1995, Reclaim the Streets halts traffic and holds a spontaneous street party on Camden High Street, London

Anti-fracking

The use of direct action in defending the environment was subsequently employed by the anti-fracking campaigns. The commercial viability of fracking has always been dependent on the prevailing price of oil as it is an expensive process – quite apart from its impact on the environment through water-table contamination and the mini-earthquakes it inevitably causes. Anti-fracking protests continued despite criminalisation of such actions. One example was the state response to actions at the Cuadrilla site at Preston New Road near Blackpool, where three protesters were sent to prison in September 2018, two for 16 months and one for 15 months. After pleading guilty, a fourth received a 12-month suspended sentence. Their action was to occupy the tops of lorries that had been part of a convoy to get drilling equipment on to the site the previous October. But over 300 people had been arrested since January 2017 after the government overruled the local council's refusal to consent to drilling, and Cuadrilla wanted to crush the opposition. In passing sentence, the judge expressed outrage that each of the defendants 'remains motivated by an unswerving confidence that they are right', adding 'even at their trial they felt justified by their actions. Given the disruption caused in this case, only immediate custody can achieve sufficient punishment.' On appeal, the three were released: the sentences were so excessive as to unnecessarily risk exposing the repressive function of the state.

In November 2019, fracking protesters won a temporary victory when the government halted fracking in England. The government report acknowledges the concerns raised by the protesters, stating:

> *'On the basis of the disturbance caused to residents living near Cuadrilla's Preston New Road site in Lancashire and this latest scientific analysis, the government has announced a moratorium on fracking until compelling new evidence is provided.'*

However, in April 2022, the government ordered a new report on fracking due to the global fuel crisis, with a view to allowing it to restart.

Anti-fracking protestors at the Cuadrilla site, near Blackpool

Stop HS2

More recently there have been actions by groups like Stop HS2. High Speed 2 is set to be a new high speed rail link from London to Birmingham and originally intended to stretch further north to Scotland. It is the single biggest ecocide project to take place on British soil, destroying 108 areas of ancient woodlands and precious habitat for endangered species across the country, as well as destroying communities and homes. The Stop HS2 campaign has brought together large numbers of tree protectors from all over the country. The Stop HS2 campaign exposed the government's phoney claims that the 'left-behind' communities of the north of England would have all their problems solved by the extension of a super-speed train line – of which the northern leg has now, anyway, been cancelled. In 2022, actions continue to take place, causing economic disruption to HS2 and highlighting that British capitalism will destroy any environment in its quest for profits.

North and East London FRFI show solidarity with the Stop HS2 mass banner drop action, February 2021

System change?

The anti-roads movement, and recent campaigns against fracking and large-scale rail development have an elementary anti-capitalist ideology. But although they were supporters of direct action, more recent movements, in particular UK Student Climate Network (UKSCN) and Extinction Rebellion (XR) did not explicitly challenge the capitalist system, deciding instead to use ambiguous language like 'system change'.

While 'system change' is presented as a criticism of the profit motive, its real purpose is to present the possibility of a capitalist future without the capitalists, in other words, a state-run capitalism, the same illusion which underpins the Green New Deal. The abstractness of the concept however fits well with XR's view that it is 'beyond politics', a stance completely at odds with the highly political source of its unbending commitment to non-violence, two ideologues of US imperialist 'soft power', Erica Chenoweth and Maria Stephan.[46]

UKSCN, an avowed supporter of a Green New Deal, called monthly student strikes from February 2019 in the wake of the appeal of Swedish climate activist Greta Thunberg and Fridays for Future; there was a huge response from school students and later university students. There was a real possibility of a serious and lasting political development among young people, but the strikes were cut short by the pandemic at the start of 2020 and UKSCN became essentially dormant, absorbed into the COP26 Coalition.

XR likewise organised significant forms of direct action involving thousands of activists. It first blockaded five London bridges in November 2018 and then occupied five points in London for two weeks in April 2019. In September 2020, XR supporters besieged printers of the tabloid press, halting their distribution and leading Home Secretary Priti Patel to describe it as an 'organised crime syndicate'. The success of XR's tactics provoked outrage among sections of the ruling class which demanded action from the Tory government; the response was sections of the Police, Crime, Sentencing and Court Act introducing severe restrictions on protests and demonstrations. Even more extreme measures were unsuccessfully introduced into the original Bill at a late stage in the Lords to criminalise actions taken by Insulate Britain. Its supporters had successfully blocked motorways and roads in November and December 2021 in a call for the installation of adequate domestic thermal insulation to reduce carbon emissions. The Green Building Council estimates

46 Robert Clough, 'A handbook of petit bourgeois vacuity', FRFI 271 August/September 2019.

FRFI join the central London Youth Strike 4 Climate / UKSCN demonstration, April 2019

that 25 million homes need insulation upgrades to meet 2050 standards. Although the extra measures in the Police, Crime, Sentencing and Court Art were defeated in the House of Lords at the time, they are now included in the government's new legislative programme.

Politically, XR came under serious challenge from very early on: it paid little heed to the disproportionate impact of climate change on underdeveloped countries; its emphasis on activists courting arrest ignored the very real oppression of the working class, especially black and Asian workers. Principles that XR put forward such as 'We avoid blaming and shaming – we live in a toxic system, but no one individual is to blame' were representative of a privileged, respectable layer which wanted an accommodation with the ruling class, with the implication that it could be won over to fighting global warming through a combination of rational argument and pressure from the 3.5% of the population whom XR thought would be prepared to get themselves arrested. UKSCN's demise was the consequence of a similar sort of elitism: a view that school students would be alienated by any explicitly anti-capitalist politics – that only a moral appeal to fighting global warming would attract their support – and that its monthly events could only be led by self-appointed organisers in closed-off online meetings.

Extinction Rebellion demonstration, Hyde Park, London, April 2019

In the 1990s and early 2000s, then, environmental campaigns put forward a basic anti-capitalist position.[47] While XR and UKSCN maintained the tradition of direct action, they distanced themselves from this standpoint. The COP26 Coalition, which has now rebranded itself as the Climate Justice Coalition, however abandoned both – and this at a time when the need for a massive anti-capitalist, direct action movement has become more and more necessary.

The recognition that 'respectable protest' has limited impact has led to more recent direct actions organised by autonomous XR groups and newly emerging campaigns like Youth Climate Swarm and Just Stop Oil. These campaigns are hitting big business where it hurts, financially. Examples include the actions against Amazon warehouses on 'Black Friday' 26 November 2021, blockading 15 Amazon warehouses in three countries preventing trade and standing with the 'Make Amazon Pay' campaign. Youth Climate Swarm and Just Stop Oil targeted oil tankers and terminals for a long weekend of action in March 2022 – causing temporary disruption to the oil distribution network, and generating outrage from representatives of the ruling class. Labour's Shadow Justice Secretary Steve Reed demanding a national injunction to prevent any repetition: 'Motorists [are] already being hammered by prices at the pump, and now millions can't even access fuel. This is all happening on the government's watch. The Conservatives need to stop standing idly by

47 'We only want the Earth – environment pull-out', FRFI 125 June/July 1995.

and put an end to this disruption that is causing misery for motorists.' UN Secretary-General António Guterres might almost have had Reed in mind when he said in April 2022 'Climate activists are sometimes depicted as dangerous radicals. But, the truly dangerous radicals are the countries that are increasing the production of fossil fuels.'[48]

Climate change is a war of the rich against the poor

From 2020, Fight Racism! Fight Imperialism! (FRFI) groups around the country built anti-capitalist, anti-imperialist environmental actions and activities, particularly through participation in Earth Strike. These highlighted in particular the role of British multinationals and British banks under the slogan 'Climate change is a war – of the rich against the poor'.

West London FRFI join Youth Climate Swarm and Just Stop Oil activists in central London, December 2021

Many FRFI groups mobilised with Earth Strike, which was launched in 2018. In London, Earth Strike North of the River launched a 'We Are Watching You' campaign around the City of London in 2018. It targeted the headquarters of many of the largest corporate polluters, the Bank of England and the

48 United Nations, 'Secretary-General Warns of climate emergency, calling Intergovernmental Panel's report "a File of Shame", while saying leaders "are lying", fuelling flames', 4 April 2022.

companies responsible for oppressing of indigenous peoples and communities. This was followed by demonstrations outside the head offices of Glencore, Unilever, BlackRock, Rio Tinto and Anglo-American. The demonstrations were collaborative events attended by a variety of organisations all of which participated on an equal, democratic basis. The key message was the need to target capitalism and imperialism by opposing the multinational corporations, banks, the investment funders and the governments whose activities are destroying the environment and threatening the future of humanity.

Environmental movements for real change

Socialists take part in struggles alongside others, arguing for democratic and open forms of organising against any elitism or sectarianism. We point out the need for the movement to defend itself and its supporters against state attack, fighting for the right to protest and supporting those arrested whether they are subsequently prosecuted or not. We stand against bans and proscriptions, supporting full participation and debate within the movement; this includes the freedom to sell progressive literature, and the right to display banners and placards on public events. We argue that the movement can only grow through building alliances with others who are fighting back against capitalism and imperialism, here and internationally. Finally, we argue that only by overthrowing capitalism and imperialism can we build a sustainable society free from environmental destruction and oppression.

North and East London FRFI putting the case for socialism, October 2021

six

SOCIALISM IS SURVIVAL

Capitalism will not collapse on its own, it still has the strength to lead us to our deaths, like airline pilots who commit suicide with their passengers. We urgently need to enter the cockpit and seize the controls together'.[49]

Only under a socialist system is there any hope that humanity can avoid a planetary catastrophe. This is a fact. The multinational corporations that dominate global production must be replaced by an economy based on production for use, not for profit, under socialist state planning. There are examples, historical and contemporary, from both the Soviet Union and Cuba that illustrate that this is the way forward. First, however, the Cold War propaganda and imperialist hostility to socialism that has triumphed in the West must be rejected. This is possible now as millions of people see the lethal realities of capitalism destroying planet Earth. The demonising ofthe USSR as indifferent to the environment in its development policies must be rejected: the success of Cuba as the most sustainable nation of the world must be accepted.

Environmental destruction under Russian Tsarism

From his detailed study of the all evidence and data collected in his 1899 work, *The Development of Capitalism in Russia*, Lenin concluded that capitalism was being established in Russia. He noted the growth of a national market for goods replacing local markets, the expansion of cash crop sowing replacing subsistence farming and increases of individual, rather than communal, property ownership. He saw an escalation

49 Serge Halimi interviewed in *L'Humanité*, 8 November 2019, republished in *Le Monde Diplomatique*, 24 March 2020.

of division amongst the peasants with a growing separation between a landholding rural bourgeoisie and a mostly landless rural proletariat recruited from a diminishing middle peasantry. The Bolshevik Party in 1917 inherited an economy of low agricultural productivity combined with an export orientated capitalism developed with great brutality under Tsarism.

The environmental impact of pre-revolutionary industrialisation under the Tsars was severe. There were no controls or limits on the rights of capitalists to pollute land and water in their pursuit of profit. Huge factories employing thousands of workers utilised oil from Baku and coal from the Donbass while the surplus was exported. Hunting for the animal fur trade and logging for wood exports devastated vast acres of forest and animal species. Russia was one of the largest cotton growing exporters in the world and the result was widespread water-logging and soil salinisation of the land which encouraged persistent malaria. In Central Asia the Tsarist regime displaced millions of nomadic herder peoples in order to free up the steppe grasslands for future exploitation.

Soviet Poster, 'Take care of the birds', 1978

An environmental protest movement of liberals and intellectuals grew throughout 19th century Russia and they are well represented in Anton Chekhov's 1899 play Uncle Vanya by the character of Doctor Astrov. He is both a physician and a part-time forest ranger who is deeply concerned about the rate of damage that industrial entrepreneurs are inflicting on the forests, and fauna and flora:

'The woods of Russia are trembling under the blows of the axe. Millions of trees have perished.

The homes of the wild animals and birds have been desolated; the rivers are shrinking, and many beautiful landscapes are gone forever... The forests are disappearing, the rivers are running dry, the game is exterminated, the climate is spoiled, and the earth becomes poorer and uglier every day'.[50]

The Russian environmentalists were not revolutionaries and they did not set out to change the mode of production but they did use their influence to develop some protective measures. In the 1890s the first *zapovedniki,* or nature reserves, were introduced into the countryside complete with experimental scientific research stations to study soil conservation methods. A new and pioneering school of bio-physicists developed ecological methods of pollution abatement on a huge scale in some of the earliest and most advanced environmental research of the time. Later, millions of hectares of natural refuges, *zakazniki*, were also established across the nation.

The environmental achievements of the revolutionary government

As documented in *Socialist States and the Environment: Lessons for Ecosocialist Futures*,[51] the Bolsheviks had an acute awareness of capitalism's inherent tendency to destroy the environment. They understood capitalism's tendency to increase productivity by intensifying the exploitation of both labour power and natural resources. Among the revolutionary government's first legislation were measures to restrict unplanned industrial output in order to protect the environment. Their communist viewpoint was the polar opposite to the rampaging 'free enterprise' ideology of the US and the colonial ruthlessness of the British Empire. From as early as 1919, controls and oversight of industrial production were enforced to protect nature. In 1921 the first agrometeorological service in the world was established. This would

50 Anton Chekhov, *Uncle Vanya*, 1899.

51 Salvatore Engel-Di Mauro, *Socialist States and the Environment: lessons for Ecosocialist futures*, Pluto Press, 2021.

later be used for climate monitoring and by 1923 wastewater legislation was enacted to protect reservoirs from sewage contamination. Forests, surface waters and underground mineral resources were all nationalised and brought under conservation policies. The All-Russian Society for the Protection of Nature was founded in 1924 and had 37 million members in 1987. Environmental education and 'mass ecological sensitisation' have been described as 'truly vast' by some commentators.[52]

State planning under socialism

The newly formed Soviet Union was a centrally planned economy in which each sector related to the centre through a variety of institutions competing for the allocation of resources. In this system the plan prevails over the market and production for social use takes precedence over the interests of private property. The state is able to action its political priorities directly without the interference of market. From the start environmental legislation and conservation measures were built into planning proposals and conformity to regulations was enforced within each sector and supervised by millions of inspectors in the People's Control Commission, which was established in 1920 as the Workers and Peasants Inspectorate.

Soviet Poster, 'Take care of Mother Nature!', 1975

Considering the circumstances in which the Revolution took place, the commitment to environmental priorities was a massive challenge. Over three million soldiers had been killed in

52 *Ibid*, p115.

the First Imperialist War and Russia's borders were blockaded by hostile imperialist armies. Human and economic devastation was on an even larger scale when the Soviet Union emerged from the Second World War in 1945 with a population loss of approximately 23 million people. The Nazi German attack with three million troops, reinforced by 30 divisions from Finland and Romania, carried-out a scorched earth strategy which destroyed most transport systems, horses and cattle. Over 25 million people were left entirely without housing, living in caves and rubble. Between 1940 and 1942, Soviet GDP fell 34%.

These were the conditions in which the Soviet state set out to rebuild its economy and feed the people.[53] Enormous strides were made in industrial production but the agricultural sector was more challenging. Several seasons of drought and flood made it difficult to grow sufficient crops and there was a famine in 1946. In 1954 the new Soviet Premier, Nikita Khrushchev, proposed the ploughing of 13 million hectares of previously uncultivated land, the so-called 'virgin soil' of Soviet Asia on the right bank of the Volga River, the northern Caucasus, western Siberia, and northern Kazakhstan.

The Virgin Lands Initiative was an ambitious attempt to put the vast semi-desert of eastern Central Asia under agricultural production and avert future food shortages for the population. The state recruited workers for the new kolkhoz (communal farms) as the opportunity for a socialist adventure for Soviet youth. During the summer of 1954, 300,000 Komsomol (Young Communist League) volunteers travelled to the Virgin Lands. Following the first successful harvest of 1954, Khrushchev raised the original target of land under cultivation to between 28-30 million hectares by 1956. The newly sown land succeeded in increasing production of grain and in alleviating food shortages. However, crop output fluctuated wildly from year to year and failed to surpass the record output of 1956. Output gradually declined

53 The great Soviet composer Dmitri Shostakovich was inspired to write *The Song of the Forests*, Op. 81, a cantata composed in the summer of 1949 to celebrate the return of nature after the devastation of war with the words, 'We will clothe our homeland with forests'.

after 1959 although remaining a vital source of food for the population.

The pioneering attempt of the Soviets to replicate the grain-producing plains of North America and Canada attracted the hostility of the West. Anti-communist propaganda increased as liberation struggles and communist parties grew around the world. It was at this Cold War moment that Khrushchev boasted that the Soviet Union would surpass the US in grain output by 1960. This was unwise because it was an unequal competition between an underdeveloped country and an advanced capitalist state. However well organised, the Soviet Union could not compete with the long-established and heavily industrialised agribusiness the US had built up since 1900.

The world was astonished when the Soviets sent the first human, Yuri Gagarin, into space in 1961, beating the US and triggering a 'space race'. But overall, the technical specialism of Soviet achievement could not compete against the western imperialist powers which were supported by the World Bank and the International Monetary Fund (IMF). The US and Britain had long established supply chains of raw material inputs from colonised regions which favoured high production and low costs. The Soviet Union was to fail in this Cold War competition after a series of drought-ridden growing seasons. In 1972, encouraged and supported by giant US farming monopolies, US President Nixon announced a three-year agreement to sell at least $750m of North American wheat, corn and other grains to the Soviet Union. This was named 'the Great Grain Robbery' by some, as global food prices rose by at least 30% the following year. This grain production 'competition' led to Khrushchev's downfall as Soviet president in 1964.

Not only were the Soviet Union's efforts to become self-sufficient in food mocked, but, additionally, reports on the environmental damage of cropping in Soviet Central Asia were seized upon. The ecological damage of intensive farming was real enough. In the area of the Aral Sea (an inland lake), dust bowl conditions like those of the Great Plains of the USA in the 1930s threatened. However, Soviet agriculturists took action, building wind breaks and other protective structures to reverse the decline in soil health. Biodiversity was encouraged and endangered species like the sturgeon and the taiga deer were protected. At the time of the collapse of the Soviet bloc in 1991, the Aral Sea was reborn in three adjacent locations and its acidity had been rebalanced.

The maintenance and restoration practices that were carried out on a huge scale by the Soviet government were possible because there was no obstruction by private companies. In contrast, US and British environmentalists face a constant fight to get the most basic information about private organisations, even where chemical spillage affects water supplies or air and soil pollution damages whole communities.

Cuba: 'From rainforest to cane field'

'As individual capitalists are engaged in production and exchange for the sake of immediate profit, only the nearest, most immediate results must first be taken into account...What cared the Spanish planters in Cuba, who burned down the forests on the slopes of the mountains and obtained from the ashes sufficient fertiliser for one generation of highly profitable coffee trees – what cared they that heavy tropical rainfall afterwards washed away the unprotected upper stratum of soil, leaving behind only bare rock! In relation to nature, as to society, the present mode of production is predominantly concerned only about the immediate, most tangible result, and then surprise is expressed that the more remote effects of actions directed to this end turn out to be quite different, are mostly quite opposite in character.'[54]

Friedrich Engels

54 Frederick Engels, *The Origin of the Family, Private Property and the State*, Lawrence & Wishart, London, 1981, p263.

Revolutionary Cuba, like the Soviet Union, inherited a degraded environment. Four hundred years of colonial and then imperialist exploitation led to chronic deforestation and soil erosion in Cuba. The expansion of the sugar industry reduced the island's forest cover from 95% pre-colonisation to 14% by the time of the Revolution in 1959, turning Cuba 'from rainforest to cane field'.[55]

Despite its early aspirations to break the chains of underdevelopment, Cuba's economy continued to be dominated by the sugar export economy. Recommendations that mechanisation and the use of chemicals would raise productivity were at first accepted in Cuba. In addition, modernising seemed to be a way forward for campesinos (farm workers and poor peasants) to relieve a lifetime of labouring on the land under the unrelenting sun. As a result of these new practices (and centuries of colonial environmental exploitation) soil erosion, water pollution and the loss of species were observed over the next decades leading inevitably to changes in the climate with more extreme droughts and flooding.

The extraordinary biodiversity and natural coastal resources of the Cuban archipelago are recognised as of global importance by the Cuban people.

Cuban pioneers contribute to the reforestation programme on the International Day of the Environment, May 2017

55 Reinaldo Funes Monzoti, speech at 'Climate Emergency - What can we learn from socialist Cuba?', meeting hosted by Rock around the Blockade, October 2019.

'Proud of our Revolution', billboard in Havana, Cuba, July 2021

After the revolution of 1959 there was an increasing concern with protecting the natural endowments of the island and, in 1976, Cuba included environmental issues in its Constitution, and the National Commission for the Protection of the Environment and the Rational Use of Natural Resources was set up. However, Cuba has a socialist state planned economy like the Soviet Union once had, and no sector was unrelated to any other. The people came to realise that the totality of production relations meant that an environmental agenda could not be separated from the rest of the political-economic framework. This comprehensive and systemic understanding of the island's needs came to the rescue of Cuba following the disintegration of the Soviet Union.

Cuba's Special Period

With the collapse of the Soviet Bloc in 1991 Cuba suddenly lost over 85% of its foreign trade and all of its oil supply. The crisis was compounded by the continuing illegal US blockade of Cuban trade. In response, the island entered what became known as a 'Special Period'. The state planned for the survival of socialism, refusing to close a single school or hospital and continuing to assert its national sovereignty. The near-collapse of the economy however resulted in a rapid fall in per capita emissions of particulate matter. Cuban environmentalists had long associated the degradation of the island's eco-system with colonial occupation, capitalist production methods and exploitative trading relations. During the Special

Period Cuba turned to organic farming, urban gardens, biodiversity and permaculture, reforestation, wind and solar power and reducing the dependency on synthetic chemicals.

The island moved to a sustainable development model which has allowed for the survival of the Revolution's social values and human development targets. In 1996, Cuba added 'sustainability' to its goals and promoted agro-ecological farming techniques nationwide.[56] An environmental perspective on all aspects of life and work was introduced, backed up by Cuba's scientific and institutional capacity and facilitated by its political-economic framework. This commitment means that today Cuba is the most environmentally sustainable country on earth.

Tarea Vida – Cuba's life project

Socialist Cuba demonstrates a successful alternative to capitalist environmental destruction. In 2006 the WWF's Living Planet Report identified Cuba as the only country in the world to have achieved sustainable development: a high level of human development coupled with a low ecological footprint. In 2015 Cuba was identified as the only country to provide a 'very high' level of human development at a cost of less than 1.7 global hectares per capita according to the Global Footprint Network and United Nations data.[57] By comparison, the average person in Britain consumes around eight global hectares, a figure which hides great inequality in consumption patterns between rich and poor. The climate emergency demands that we learn from Cuba's history and the goals it sets itself today to create a fair, sustainable society.

On 30 June 2019, Cuba experienced its hottest day on record, reaching a searing 39.1°C in the town of Veguitas in the eastern province of Granma. With the hurricane season increasing in intensity each year, bringing greater costs in human life and to the economy, the effects of climate

56 Helen Yaffe, *We Are Cuba! How a revolutionary people have survived in a post-soviet world*, 2020, p62.

57 Global Footprint Network, 'Only eight countries meet two key conditions for sustainable development', 23 September 2015.

Cuban's working on their organopónico on the 20th Anniversary of the Programme for Urban Agriculture, Cienfuegos, Cuba, 2017. An organopónico is an organic, urban farm.

change are hitting the Cuban people. Under a tightening US blockade and facing rising sea levels and temperatures, socialist Cuba is responding to scarcity and climate change by putting humanity first.

In Britain, coastal villages under threat from erosion and rising sea levels are being abandoned by the state. The residents of Fairbourne in North Wales, for example, have been told the government is under no obligation to compensate them for their forced displacement or the collapse in the market value of their homes caused by the changing climate.[58] Compare this to Cuba, where in April 2017 the government approved Life Task (Tarea Vida): State Plan for Tackling Climate Change, a 100-year plan to protect the island and its population from the effects of global warming. Preparations have already begun; for the threatened settlement of Tunas de Zaza-Médano in Sancti Spiritus province, the state has started looking for alternative locations, taking into account the jobs and customs of the inhabitants.[59]

Cuba's Life Task plan consists of five strategic actions and 11 tasks. It starts with identifying risk, vulnerable areas and predicted effects then sets out actions to be taken to mitigate them.

58 Tom Wall, '"This is a wake-up call": the villagers who could be Britain's first climate refugees', *The Guardian*, 18 May 2019.

59 Escambray, 3 March 2019

- Prohibit construction of new housing in vulnerable coastal settlements under threat of disappearing due to flooding and receding coastlines. Reduce population density in low-lying coastal areas.
- Adapt infrastructure in low-lying coastal zones to the threat of floods.
- Adapt agricultural activities, in particular those with the greatest impact on the country's food security, to changes in land use as a result of sea level rise and drought.
- Reduce crop areas near the coast or affected by saline intrusion. Diversify crops, improve soil conditions, develop and introduce varieties resistant to rising temperatures.
- Set deadlines for planning processes of relocation of threatened settlements and infrastructure, in accordance with the country's economic conditions. Start with lower cost measures, such as induced natural solutions (beach recovery and reforestation).
- Tarea Vida is incorporated into all areas of Cuban society.

Tarea Vida incorporates a programme of progressive investments categorised into short- (2020), medium- (2030), long- (2050) and very long-term (2100). The plan focuses on disaster reduction by using the country's scientific capacity to reduce the danger, vulnerability and territorial risk.

The Cuban government has not wasted time in fulfilling the ecological commitments of the new Constitution approved in 2019. On 14 July of that year, Cuba's National Assembly signed in a new fisheries law with provisions to curtail illegal fishing, preserve coral reefs, recover fish populations and protect small-scale fisheries drawing on the expertise of scientists, conservationists and coastal communities. The government has also announced that it would conduct a one-year trial in Havana of distributing subsidised 90-litre solar-powered water heaters, manufactured in Cuba, for use in residential buildings.[60] If successful, the scheme can be rolled out nationally to further reduce energy consumption.

60 *Juventud Rebelde*, 27 August 2019.

Humanity's 'Special Period'

Cuba has overcome immense challenges. It survived the collapse of its main trading partner the Soviet Union; it is surviving a 60-year US blockade and constant imperialist aggression; on top of this it has made world-leading advances in environmental sustainability. It has been able to do so thanks to its socialist planned economy and workers' state. This is a lesson for environmental movements across the world as humanity is faced with its own 'Special Period' of reduced consumption forced by decades of inaction on climate change. We can no longer afford to sustain a bloated, parasitic ruling class. We must rapidly reorganise society along sustainable lines. The Cuban Revolution demonstrates the need to overthrow capitalism in order to achieve this system change. There is a need for urgency. In May 2022, *The Guardian* reported that:

- The fossil fuel industry's short-term expansion plans involve the start of oil and gas projects that will produce greenhouse gases equivalent to a decade of CO_2 emissions from China, the world's biggest polluter.
- These plans include 195 gigantic oil and gas projects that would each result in at least a billion tonnes of CO_2 emissions over their

Hitching and bicycles, Havana, Cuba 1995

lifetimes, in total equivalent to about 18 years of current global CO_2 emissions. About 60% of these have already started pumping.

- The dozen biggest oil companies are on track to spend $103m a day for the rest of the decade exploiting new fields of oil and gas that cannot be burned if global heating is to be limited to well under 2°C.
- The scale of these projects is such that they would swallow up the entire world's budget of 646Gt CO_2 emissions, and would imperil even the achievement of a global temperature rise of 2.7°C let alone 1.5°C or 2°C.
- Shell and BP are both in the top ten companies for level of investment in new oil or gas sources.[61]

At the Rio de Janeiro UN Earth Summit 30 years ago, Fidel Castro urged world leaders to take action: 'Unequal trade, protectionism and the foreign debt assault the ecological balance and promote the destruction of the environment. If we want to save humanity from this self-destruction, wealth and available technologies must be distributed better throughout the planet...Enough of selfishness. Enough of schemes of domination. Enough of insensitivity, irresponsibility and deceit.' Capitalism is indeed leading to our extinction and we must turn to socialism as our only means of survival. We need to defend the example of Cuba, not just for Cuba's sake but for the future of humankind. The global dominance of imperialism will be the death knell of humanity – it is already killing millions, depriving millions more of the basic means of survival and forcing millions into displacement from their homes and into refugee camps. During 2020, 82.4 million people were forcibly displaced worldwide as a result of war, famine, ecological disaster, persecution and violence.[62]

The productive capacity in the world today is sufficient to produce the basic material needs of food, housing, access to clean water and sewerage for the whole population of the world. Yet still today some 2.2 billion people do not have safely managed drinking water services, 4.2 billion do

---

61 Damian Carrington and Matthew Taylor, 'Revealed: the "carbon bombs" set to trigger catastrophic climate breakdown', *The Guardian*, 11 May 2022.

62 UNHCR, Global Trends Report, June 2022.

Newcastle FRFI, COP26 demonstration, September 2021

not have safely managed sanitation services, and three billion lack basic handwashing facilities. Nearly one in three people (2.37 billion) did not have access to adequate food in 2020. Although it is technically possible to meet these unfulfilled needs, under the capitalist system no profit can be extracted from doing so.

Socialism – the only way

Socialism means planned national development, not the pursuit of private profit, but in the interests of the population and environment as a whole. Rationalising production to replace capitalist consumerism will provide the socialist solution to an equitable future where the Earth's natural resources are respected as part of the equation of production and nurtured for future generations. Natural resources like land, water, raw materials and hydrocarbons must be used sustainably as part of a harmonious whole. A leading environmental policy maker in Cuba pointed out that the process 'is not automatic, you have to try to create a socialist system where the environmental agenda is driven well, otherwise you will still have environmental problems. Nothing is given, it has to be achieved.'[63] In this spirit the Cuban people have pioneered a way forward that offers the possibility of slowing down the climate crisis, producing food for the population and utilising sustainable methods of production.

The fight for climate justice must go hand-in-hand with the fight for social justice if we are to project Cuba's experiences on a world scale. In the documentary film *Cuba's Life Task: Combatting Climate Change* Orlando Rey, lead negotiator for Cuba at COP26 and Climate Advisor in Cuba's Ministry of Science states that:

> *'There is a risk in trying to solve climate issues from a climate perspective, ignoring the socio-economic premises which create these problems. Structural problems must be solved... it is very difficult in conditions of poverty or deep economic and social inequality to advance a climate agenda. There must be a change in the way of life, in our aspirations... it requires a vision not directed towards profit or self-interest. It must be premised on social equity and rejecting inequity. A plan of this nature requires a different social system, and that is socialism.'*[64]

We must join Cuba, seize the power from capitalism and pilot humanity to survival. As Fidel Castro warned at the Rio Earth Summit in 1992, 'Tomorrow it will be too late to do what should have been done a long time ago.'

Join Fight Racism! Fight Imperialism! on the streets and in our communities to fight for the environment, to fight for our future. Capitalism is extinction. Socialism is survival!

---

63 Helen Yaffe, op cit, p100.

64 Helen Yaffe, Daniesky Acosta, Hugo Rivalta, *Cuba's Life Task: Combatting Climate Change*, 2021.

Liverpool FRFI led an anti-imperialist bloc on the COP26 coalition march, November 2021

Bulk orders of this pamphlet

You can help to get this pamphlet widely circulated by ordering bulk copies. .

☐ 5 for £14.95 (inc P&P)

☐ 10 for £24.95 (inc P&P)

☐ 20 for £39.95 (inc P&P)

We hope that it will lead to reading groups in schools, colleges, universities, workplaces and communities. It is so important that the environmental movement adopts an anti-imperialist position and discusses the example of socialist Cuba to show that another world is possible!

Send cheques payable to Larkin Publications to
FRFI, BCM Box 5909, London WC1N 3XX together with your postal adress.
You can also pay via PayPal: donations@rcgfrfi.plus.com

Order more copies of our publications

To order any of our pamphlets or books go to

www.revolutionarycommunist.com/books

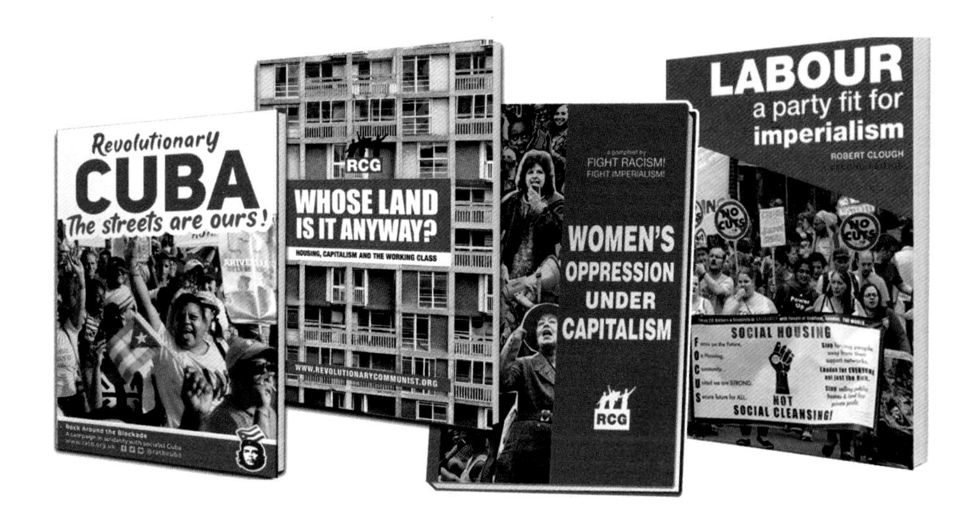

Subscribe to

FIGHT RACISM! FIGHT IMPERIALISM!

www.REVOLUTIONARYCOMMUNIST.org

Keep up to date with our analysis. Subscribe to FRFI and visit our website!

FRFI subscription rates: (please tick ☐)

	Biritain inc N.Ireland	Europe (air)	World (air PPR)	World (air sealed)
1 year	☐ £8.50	☐ £12.00	☐ £13.50	☐ £21.00
2 year	☐ £16.00	☐ £22.50	☐ £26.00	☐ £40.00

Take out an additional subsciption for a prisoner: 1 year ☐ £15.00 2 years ☐ £40.00

Cheques payable to Larkin Publications. Please add £5 for non-sterling cheques.

☐ I would like to subscribe to Fight Racism! Fight Imperialism! beginning with issue ________

☐ and a sub for a prisoner beginning with issue ________

Name ____

Address ____

____

I enclose payment of £ ______________

Please return to FRFI BCM Box 5909, London WC1N 3XX

or pay via PayPal at donations@rcgfrfi.plus.com